Mercy

A Memoir of Medical Trauma
and True Crime Obsession

Published by Barrelhouse Books
Baltimore, MD

www.barrelhousemag.com

Published in the United States of America

ISBN 13: 978-0-9889945-7-7

First Edition

Cover design: Shanna Compton
Page design: Adam Robinson

A MEMOIR OF MEDICAL TRAUMA & TRUE CRIME OBSESSION

mercy

Marcia Trahan

For Andy, the other star in my sky

Contents

Chapter 1

Murder Nights

L ate at night, when I'm bored or broken or raging inside, I bring out the snacks and turn on true crime TV.

Like the players in the clear-cut moral universe of Investigation Discovery programs and *Forensic Files*, my favorite sources of gore, the food is either wholly bad (sugary, salty, fattening) or wholly good (organic, rich in nutrients).

I tend to skip meals on busy days. By ten p.m., I'm ravenous. Standing in the kitchen, I pack away calories during commercial breaks. Back on the sofa, before things get messy onscreen, I perch on the edge of the cushion, gulping soy milk and crunching handfuls of Lay's potato chips. Squeamishness and guilt prevent me from eating while crime scenes are on display. Once thawed, frozen strawberries look like guts, squishy and limp in their ruby-red puddle of juice. And shoveling forkfuls of apple pie straight from the tin feels like mocking the dead: *I'm scarfing junk food, and you can't have any.*

Next to my stack of unread books, a table lamp provides the only light in the room, except for the quick-edit flashes from the TV.

The moment the corpse appears, I go from consuming to being consumed.

I am electrified by the sight of stab wounds and ligature marks. My heart beats faster, harder. I let in the violence that seeks my violence, devours the sorrowing anger I can only feel in the dark.

Sometimes, I take a throw pillow and lie back on the carpet in front of the screen, my field of vision filled with the larger-than-life world of the dead.

While I'm devouring and being devoured, Andy, my partner, is upstairs, reading in bed: DeLillo, Pynchon, a profile of Nixon, or a history of the Vietnam War. The pile of books that waits for me includes doctors' memoirs, volumes of poetry, and works of literary criticism.

We could be mistaken for a pair of snooty intellectuals, the kind of insufferable couple who try to outdo each other with witticisms and obscure references until one finally wins, and the other leaves for someone younger and dumber. But flanked by tall, crammed bookshelves, our TV sits at the center of the wall opposite the sofa. We turn it off when Andy's guitar students come by, when we have guests for dinner, when he's out doing errands and I'm upstairs editing, or when I'm reading before bed. Otherwise, it is always on.

Andy and I were both anxious children, growing up with alcoholic parents in the 1970s and '80s. We needed to see how people might live in situations not painfully circumscribed by addiction. How families could be. Television excited us, soothed us, revealed to us the world of functioning adults. Images, faces, and voices assured us we were not alone.

Now middle-aged, we still use TV to meet our needs for connection, though what we connect to is sometimes different. Andy is a news and weather junkie: if there's a hurricane or an out-of-control wildfire or, you know, some madman running for public office, he wants to hear all about it, can't bear to reprise his role as the younger brother left out of the loop. A career depressive, I limit my news intake. I crave death at night, but I can't afford to immerse myself for long in today's mayhem, broadcast live.

During afternoon breaks, at dinnertime, and in the early evening, Andy and I watch reruns of sitcoms. At ten, Andy heads upstairs, leaving the living room to me. In our first years together, we read side by side in bed before turning out the light. In the months after I was treated for thyroid cancer, I told Andy I needed time alone to read or do yoga or write in my journal before trying to fall asleep. He balked at first, but he couldn't do much except retreat, nurse his rejection for a while, and eventually come to appreciate uninterrupted Internet sessions in my office and the quiet of our spare, white-walled bedroom.

I did not tell him I also needed time alone to cry, or to curl up on the sofa staring at the carpet, struggling to figure out what came next after *empty*.

More than a decade after the cancer, he knows what I do on certain nights, in the hours that mark the edge between one day and the next.

True crime death is not what often passes for death on *Law & Order*: some model-actress resting elegantly in a pool of what looks like raspberry puree, carefully made up to appear bruised. It's much more real, much more gruesome—though not gruesome enough for a voyeur like me. The level of realness varies. Network newsmagazine shows like *20/20* and *Dateline*, which perpetually rerun on Investigation Discovery (ID) and the Oprah Winfrey Network (OWN), use courtroom footage as well as interviews with police, lawyers, accused and convicted perpetrators, victims' tearful family members, and the occasional survivor. They display crime scene photos as heavily pixelated blurs, disturbing to me in their own way for what is left to my imagination.

ID's original programs, like *Deadly Women* and *Fatal Vows*, don't pretend to be news. The act of murder and the unveiling of its aftermath are portrayed in stylized recreated scenes that might seem like *Law & Order* at first glance, but the violence tends to be more explicit and the crime scenes bloodier. The actors are not the polished performers of dramatic series, nor are they models; they resemble the ordinary people they're portraying. But the face of an ID corpse is still that of an actor playing dead.

Most ID shows are presented in hour-long episodes. On *Forensic Files*, a program on the CNN network HLN (formerly Headline News), they only have half an hour, so they get right to the point. These stories *were* news, after all, and I suppose the brisk manner of storytelling preserves the illusion for many viewers that this is *still* news, not entertainment, as if that were a meaningful distinction. Recreations are brief and minimalistic. The show's distinguishing feature is the use of actual crime scene photos that display the mess left by frenzy: Blood in every shade from crimson to carmine, fresh and partly dried and long dried, splashes and puddles, trickles and specks. Bodies with splayed limbs and gunshot wounds shown clearly. But even here, the faces are pixelated, their goggle-eyed expressions presumably too much to take.

Whether I'm watching an actor or staring at an evidence photo, I want to see the faces of the dead. I want to see myself in them. Once, long ago, I nearly died by my own hand. After that, diseases threatened my life, and the treatment of those diseases felt like being brought to the edge of death.

I could have been a corpse on the autopsy table. But I'm not looking for just any dead body. No matter which show I'm watching, I'm looking for women murdered by men. I need to see dead woman after dead woman. I need to imagine myself in their places. I need to be silenced with guns, hammers, ropes, knives. Especially knives. Again and again.

I study the aftermath—the female body grievously wounded, stilled by a man. And then I have to see the bad man pay. The killer hunted down, trapped, and locked up forever.

When my interest in true crime TV became an obsession, I didn't realize that these stories are wildly popular with women. It's astonishing to me that I didn't immediately notice all the ads for diapers, laundry detergent, and dating websites. But I was too guilt-ridden over my entertainment choices to think clearly about other viewers. I thought I was a freak; to the extent that I considered my fellow viewers at all, I assumed only other weirdos would watch this stuff. I didn't especially want to find people like me, preoccupied with autopsies and blood spatter analysis. I thought I had to watch alone in the dark.

I was years into my obsession before I began to wonder about the people who shared it. I was relieved when I found 2015 Nielsen data indicating that ID was the top cable network among women ages twenty-five to fifty-four, plus dozens of articles analyzing the overwhelming popularity of true crime TV, books, and podcasts among female consumers. Maybe I wasn't quite such a freak after all.

Theories about true crime TV's appeal to its female audience abound. One explanation is that plots frequently center on domestic trouble. Here, no bond is sacred: Women kill and are killed by lovers, husbands, even sisters and female friends. Mothers kill their own children, and teenagers kill their own mothers. Fathers kill entire families. Our culture's promises of love, marriage, and motherhood as sources of uncomplicated happiness are exposed as fairytale illusions—the very illusions that are sold right back to us during commercials.

Some women viewers may simply enjoy the soap-operatic drama of these stories. Others view them as something much deeper than entertainment. Crime fiction writer Megan Abbott links the revelations of the #MeToo movement with the popularity of true crime and crime fiction books among women in a 2018 article for the *Los Angeles Times*, stating that both genres provide a "place where women can go to read about the dark, messy stuff of their lives," to work through the traumas they often suffer in silence. In my view, true crime TV offers women the same opportunity to explore trauma through stories of domestic violence, stalking, and sexual assault.

But true crime TV isn't solely about identifying with victims. It allows us to witness the strength of survivors, to see justice at work, and to explore the vengeful impulses most of us never act on. The testimony of survivors helps to convict rapists. The relentless efforts of prosecutors send murdering husbands to prison. Women are sometimes perpetrators, and they are both fascinating and relatable.

It's also important to remember that some women's preoccupation with true crime may stem from factors more complex than a desire for justice, revenge, or validation. In *Savage Appetites*, journalist Rachel Monroe points out that women become obsessed with crime stories for reasons as varied as women themselves, due to differences in psychological makeup and idiosyncratic curiosities. Their motives may be multifaceted and may not be apparent to observers. I consider my own reasons to be a mix of the straightforward and the complicated. I love seeing criminals get caught. I'm interested in troubled families. And I carry with me a tangle of fears that date back to childhood, a certain degree of personal darkness, and an array of experiences that permanently marked me though they aren't as obviously traumatic as rape.

When I was thirty-five, my thyroid was removed in two surgeries, three weeks apart—first one half of the gland, in which they found cancer, and then the other half, in which they correctly assumed there was also cancer. To my eyes, the twice-opened incision at the base of my throat didn't look as if my grandfatherly surgeon had performed an act of mercy. It looked like he'd tried to kill me. Yet I had given my consent for the procedures. The surgeon had *saved* my life. I couldn't understand why I didn't feel grateful toward him. How could I be angry at him? Why did I feel unsafe in my body after the cancer was gone?

When I developed blood clots in my leg and lungs, I gave my consent for additional procedures at the hands of male practitioners. Again, I felt invaded. Threatened even more by the treatment than by the disease itself.

Sometime after this second round of interventions, I found myself drawn to true crime television—to the most horrifying stories of women brutalized, women's lives extinguished. Stories of sexual assault followed by murder answered a particular urgency, a fury in me that cried out to be vanquished. Before my medical procedures, I'd avoided explicitly violent TV and film content. I had long been a *Law & Order* fan, but that program's more graphic episodes prompted me to turn the channel. The show's promo spots touted episodes that were "ripped from the headlines," making me uncomfortably aware that there were real-life counterparts to the fictional crimes. The unrealistic pools of blood were at that time plenty real to me.

I was especially unnerved by stories of murders involving sexual assault. It seemed to me that such episodes catered to men with sick fantasies, yet these stories were often written by women. I wondered why beautiful young actresses were willing to play the violated dead on autopsy tables, clad only in sheets, or to portray tough-talking detectives, trading quips with their male counterparts over the shapely, motionless bodies.

Ignorant of the challenges—and the horrors—women faced in Hollywood, I couldn't understand why so many participated in the desecration of their gender. It was as if they had never lain awake, alone, thinking that the faint, mysterious noise they could barely make out was the sound of their front door's lock being picked. Never mistakenly perceived a man's figure in a darkened corridor as they frantically felt for a light switch. Never imagined that they would suffer through unspeakable acts in their last moments alive. But then I had always feared being raped by an intruder to a degree other women found excessive.

When I was a teenager, my mother unwittingly terrified me with details of rape and murder from the true crime books she read avidly. She did not intend these to be cautionary tales—she shared them with me because she needed an audience. Mom was a lonely housewife, her life further constricted by addiction and by the chronic illnesses that plagued her for decades. I begged her not to fill my head with images of shootings, knife attacks, and sexual assaults, but she would not be denied. She had to tell someone. She was hooked on the violence that enlivened her days as surely as she was dependent on alcohol. In the '80s, there were no 24-7 crime networks on TV, few programs with melo-dramatic narrators to draw you into a world of death, to make you feel you weren't completely alone in your lurid tastes. My mother had to get her fix through the silence of text. Ann Rule, with her precisely detailed psychological studies of criminals and her blood-soaked descriptions of their crimes, was Mom's favor-ite author.

Once I was deep into my own true crime obsession, I began to understand why she so urgently needed to relate these tales. I wanted to tell someone about the strangely captivating images of ruin I absorbed in the late-night hours, the same hours my mother had devoted to drinking and watching old sitcoms. But I was much too ashamed to tell anyone of my viewing habits, even Andy. Had my mother been alive, I would have discussed with her the scientific breakthroughs of *Forensic Files*, the love triangles of ID's *Deadly Sins*. I would have felt guilty about shar-ing my enjoyment of other women's tragedies, but I don't think I would have been able to resist making that connection with her. I had grown up believing my mother and I had nothing in common, and only learned differently after she was gone.

But if my mother planted the seeds of my obsession, why did that obsession take two decades to emerge?

Since I was a young child, Mom suffered from gastrointestinal conditions that required invasive, painful procedures. Today, I imagine asking her if she thought her many tests and surgeries led to her fascination with criminal bloodshed. She was not an introspective person. I think she would have rolled her eyes at the very idea.

My mother's relentlessly self-examining daughter couldn't see how crime linked to medicine either, not for years.

Chapter 2

Little Mysteries

Throughout my childhood, my mother kept vanishing. Mysterious illnesses took her away to the hospital from the time I was nine: a gynecological problem for which a hysterectomy was deemed the solution, followed by diverticulitis and another inflammatory condition diagnosed first as colitis and then as Crohn's disease. She drank herself into a ghost every night of my adolescence. In the last years of her life, I became a semi-dutiful daughter, calling her weekly; I must have sensed that we had little time left. She died when she was sixty-six and I was twenty-nine, her already compromised body fatally weakened by surgery.

The silence of her absence allows me to begin to understand her life.

I have always seen my mother from a distance. From the beginning, we were torn apart. Three and a half weeks before my mother's due date, a scalpel freed me from her womb as it had freed her last two babies. She went into labor early; perhaps her thirty-six-year-old body was ready to get this over with, the birth of a fifth unplanned child. Or perhaps I was restless, eager to see what the world was all about. I wonder if she felt rejected by me, or I by her.

A knife ended her final pregnancy and began my life beyond her. It cut the umbilical cord, separating us.

We were patients before we were mother and daughter. I was a preemie, though hardly a dangerously early arrival; once cleaned of my mother's blood, I had to be checked over for defects, signs of distress. Meanwhile, her belly had to be stitched up.

I wonder now: How long before she held me for the first time? What if the surgeon had placed me on my mother's chest, moments after he cut the cord through which she had fed me for eight months, creating my first scar? Would I have spent most of the next twenty-nine years asking, *How did I come from you?* Would she have spent those years after we were prematurely cleaved asking, *How did you come from me?*

The overburdened mother is a frequent figure in true crime TV. Surprise pregnancies prompt the men in these shows to either propose marriage or get out of town, unless the woman is his mistress and his solution to the problem is murder. Women tend to believe that marriage will mark the beginning of the best part of their lives, family-centered years filled with the love and prosperity shown in commercials for diamond jewelry and high-capacity washing machines. But in true crime, weddings, whether elaborate or hasty affairs, are the point at which the countdown to trouble begins.

Postpartum depression is the villain in some stories. On an episode of *Deadly Women*, a mother of four young children suffers from a particularly severe version of the disorder, becoming sicker after the birth of each baby. A devout Baptist, she finally seeks help from her pastor, who tells her she doesn't need medication, she just needs to pray more. One night, she loses control and sets the family's house on fire, killing herself, her husband, and two of their children.

It's an extreme case, but it reminds me of the terrible power of depression, reminds me to be vigilant toward my disease. I hope that stories like this one prompt women who need help to get psychiatric care. I feel better about watching true crime TV when I consider what it might offer to other women who struggle alone with their pain. It helps me to understand my own experiences—things no one in my life can help me to fathom. True crime books helped my mother forget her loneliness, and fed the very real desire for darkness that quite possibly stemmed from her own medical ordeals.

But my mother wasn't yet reading true crime when I came along, so she didn't have that release, that strange solace. The demands of cooking and cleaning for a large family plus caring for a newborn would have consumed all of her time and energy. It's the energy I wonder about. Just how much strength did she have for three a.m. feedings and endless diaper changes? Did this new baby chip away at her physical and emotional resources? Did she despair, like certain overburdened mothers of true crime?

The only female perpetrator I remember from my mother's true crime stories is Diane Downs. In her book about Downs, *Small Sacrifices*, Ann Rule describes in riveting, merciless detail how Downs shot her three young children in the chest as they sat in her car, and was convicted of murdering her seven-year-old daughter and attempting to murder her eight-year-old daughter and three-year-old son. I know all of the details now after reading the book myself.

Small Sacrifices was a library volume, a hardcover, when my mother first read it, which indicates she wasn't content to wait a year to purchase an affordable paperback edition. My mother talked about this book with more pleasure and at greater length than any other book. She told me about this crime the way she told me about the others: against my protests.

"And she did it for a *man*," my mother said, eyes bright, leaning forward in the recliner while I tried to do my tenth-grade homework on the sofa. "She had this boyfriend who didn't want kids. So she shot them!"

I squirmed. "Mom, you know I really don't like to hear about these things—"

"*Her own children!*" I can still hear her saying it. I didn't know how to describe the tone of her voice. It disturbed me. I sensed that she meant to sound horrified, but her tone wasn't one of horror. I now recognize it as one of excitement. It was a story she hadn't waited to read, couldn't wait to talk about.

I don't believe my mother knew about the concept of the unconscious mind. I think she would have scoffed at the idea that Downs's terrible act represented her own fantasy on a level far below awareness, a fantasy that might appeal to any woman who felt burdened by motherhood, even if she would never intentionally harm her children.

A mother who had tried to do her best could forgive herself for her failings when she read of Downs's crime. My mother voiced her anger at her children but never physically acted on it. Her rage was a tension that never broke.

I think another part of this story's appeal for Mom was the fact that, for once, the woman wasn't the victim.

My parents, both from families of ten children each, married after a few months of dating, when my mother discovered she was pregnant. In photographs taken before I was born, my parents sit on opposite ends of a sofa with a row of plump babies between them. My mother is pale, dark-haired, and very thin, determinedly smiling a bright-red-lipsticked smile. My father is pale, dark-haired, and skinny, too, but solemn. Every year, for four years, another baby. With each one, the distance between the man and the woman grows wider.

These skinny people were my siblings' parents. I would know them as potbellied, but still with slender limbs. My father's face grew ruddy over time from drinking. On workdays, he wore a light blue button-down shirt, gray slacks, and a dark blue tie, a confining ensemble he loathed; on weekends, he wore soft white T-shirts and loose jeans to tend the garden. My mother stayed pale, applied her red lipstick whenever she left the house, and turned from curlers to perms in a decades-long battle to give shape to her short, straight hair.

After delivering three daughters and a son, my mother defied Catholic doctrine and went on the pill, still a relatively new invention in 1964.

"Those priests would have wanted me to have more kids, like my mother," Mom said later. "Those *men*. What, I was supposed to have babies to please them? What the hell did they know about it, anyway?"

To my knowledge, she did not get pregnant again until a delayed trip to the drugstore for a birth control refill led to my conception, almost six years after the birth of my next-oldest sibling.

All of my mother's previous babies were full-term. I came very late in her reproductive life and arrived almost a month early, a double surprise for a family with scant emotional and financial resources. My father was then struggling to keep his farm machinery business going and stay current with the mortgage and other debts. Mom worked morning to evening, keeping the two-story house clean and orderly amid the boisterous games of her young kids. It might have been a little easier for her if I were not different from the beginning: born at five pounds, eight ounces, the smallest of her children. Back then, an early delivery by caesarean warranted a week in our small-town Vermont hospital for mother and baby. I lost weight during my first days of life.

"You were just five pounds when we brought you home," Mom liked to say. "You were like a little sack of sugar. I couldn't find clothes to fit you! Even the things for newborns were too small."

A sweet little mystery who didn't fit. Born early. Born late.

I believe that both my parents suffered from lifelong undiagnosed depression, and used alcohol to self-medicate. Little is known about the genetic basis for depression, but it does run in families. Researchers believe that both genes and environment factor into the risk of developing the disease. I would grow depressed in my early teens, finally and unmistakably becoming my parents' child beyond physical resemblance, but in a way they didn't want to acknowledge.

I have long wondered if my mother had postpartum depression after I was born. If there are photos of her cradling her little sack of sugar, they are missing from my family album and from my memory. I have no photographic proof that we bonded soon after the separation of the C-section. No photos at all from my first month of life.

There are no photos of my father holding me as a baby, either. My father viewed his parental responsibility as beginning and ending with earning money to support us. He suffered under the stress of providing for a large family. Three years after my birth, my father's business failed, and we lost our house, something my mother never forgave; they somehow managed to buy a small ranch home in a rural part of town. My father then turned to selling cars, a high-pressure job he loathed but stuck with nearly all of his adult life. He enjoyed his kids' company for his favorite activities, like gardening and fishing, but my mother would bitterly complain that he never helped with childcare.

Later, in my baby book, Mom would write entire pages about my first years of school, all in her elegant cursive handwriting with its startlingly severe right-side slant. But when I was a newborn, she recorded only the date, time, and place of my birth, and she must have pushed herself to compose the long list of baby gifts she received from relatives. She made no mention of the C-section, probably thinking it an unseemly thing to note.

She wrote little else about my infant and toddler years, leaving many pages blank. I see exhaustion in those spaces.

She liked to brag about how my sisters changed my diapers and gave me my bottle. I imagine my three sisters, ages ten, nine, and six, eager to help Mom when she looked pale and tired, caring for an infant when they should have been playing with dolls. It was a great deal for them to give so young. They were learning to see me as a surrogate child. I became dependent on them, only to see them grow up and begin leaving home while I was still a little girl. We would never know how to simply be siblings, equals.

The stressed mother of true crime is often a sympathetic figure. She is seen cradling her aching head while a child wails in the background, frantically punching buttons on a calculator next to a stack of bills while her husband downs beer after beer. Sometimes she manages to pull things together, with or without the father's help. If she decides instead to vent her rage at her husband and kids, she suddenly becomes a scary character. If the man vents his rage, too, their home becomes a war zone. We fear for the children.

My mother tried to make our little ranch house with its white aluminum siding as pretty and comfortable as the green wood-sided house we had lost, saving what she could over time from the grocery money to redecorate. She bought a new plaid sofa, drapes, and a plush carpet, all in shades of rust and cream, for the living room. She painted the master bedroom lemon yellow, hung wallpaper with delicate river scenes over the shrill turquoise paint in the stairwell leading to the basement. In her mind, it never measured up to our old house, that mythic fulfilment of her modest dreams.

When my mother was angry, which she was most days, she was loud. Like a man. She yelled at my father. She fought with my sisters. I played and read alone in my room or outside. Alone was easier, although I could still hear. My mother's voice filled our little house. She didn't yell at me as much. When she did, the sky split and her rage was my atmosphere. My tears made her angrier, but the guilt made her stop.

My father was quiet until he wasn't, his temper flaring without warning. When he yelled, the air was gasoline waiting for a match. Whoever had dropped the tennis racket clattering on the kitchen floor or failed to finish their glass of milk at dinner froze, confounded by his reaction to the minor crime.

Only his loud voice frightened me when I was little. Later, it would be his stare, his smirk, his slurred words, his unpredictable body.

Our parents didn't hit us. Except for the "one good spanking" my father gave each of us very young, so good we never needed another. Except for the time I saw my father slap one of my sisters hard across the face, for mouthing off to him. Except for Mom's story about one night when it was just her and my father and my oldest sister, then three months old. The baby wouldn't stop crying in the middle of the night. My father got up. At twenty-one, he knew nothing about quieting babies. I wonder if he was drinking then. I wonder why I'm looking for some way to excuse his reaching into the crib and slapping his infant daughter. Mom leaped up and pushed him away, hard.

Our parents didn't hit us.

As I approached school age, I think my mother found me an odd child: obedient but intense, drawn too deeply into my own world, always reading or drawing or acting out the elaborate stories I invented for my dolls and stuffed animals. She was at once mystified by my imagination and thankful that I could play independently for hours.

"Marcia can always entertain herself," she told relatives proudly.

Mom had plenty of hugs and kisses to give, and usually

caved into my whispered requests for candy bars and cheap toys when I accompanied her on errands, but she had no energy for children's games. I don't know if it occurred to her that I had to create a vivid, sustaining aloneness. In our rural isolation, at the end of a dirt road, only one boy my age lived close enough to be a playmate.

I was not simply shy: I was frightened by almost anything that was unfamiliar, any uncertainty. At school, I wept inconsolably when the teacher led us into the adjoining classroom for reading time, and again when she rearranged our desks in the main classroom into groups of four; I understood my place in a row but not in a cluster.

I don't know if I was more fearful than my siblings had been. I only know that Mom seemed confounded by my anxieties and tearful meltdowns, as if this degree of sensitivity was new to her. Or perhaps it was uncomfortably familiar. She had been a shy, nervous child, and was now a shy, nervous, middle-aged woman. These were not traits any mother wants to pass on.

"Why are you getting all upset?" she would ask, looking puzzled and sometimes annoyed. I never knew how to explain it to her.

I often hid in my room when neighbors or relatives visited. I had trouble falling asleep, worried that I would forget to bring a book or project to school and face humiliation, as if the gentle, patient women who taught me would ever intentionally shame a child; afraid of the ghosts and black-haired beasts that lurked in my closet, under my bed, in the thick woods at the edges of the cow pastures all around our house; afraid that my father would stumble and crash through my bedroom door, that my mother would scream at him for it.

I don't remember exactly when the drunkwalks began to happen every night; they happened often when I was young, and became nightly occurrences sometime during my high school years. My father was always the more impaired of the two. I lay in bed, listening to my mother dragging him up the stairs, down the hall, closer and closer to my room at the end. I held my breath as she got him into the bathroom that was next to my room, heard his splashing piss, his elbows banging the door frame, heard my mother growling that he'd better not fall. I heard his soft, murmuring vodka protest lullaby, his stumbling in his deerskin slippers, knees hitting corners, palms smacking doors until he made it across the hall from the bathroom to my parents' bedroom on the other side of my wall, the springs in their mattress crying out from the dead weight of his drop.

On alert, waiting for my father's drinking to lead to dire injury and counting on it to provoke my mother's rage, I was especially sensitive to beings who threatened to tear the night.

A TV-movie trailer could give me nightmares: A knockoff of *Rosemary's Baby* featured a carriage with skeletal adult-size hands hanging over the sides. Another knockoff, this one of *Psycho*, showed an old woman's shrunken head. But I was most afraid of Bigfoot, who did not look to my eyes like a man in an ape costume, but like the kind of creature who might emerge from the woods, leading a string of monsters including that thing in the baby carriage and the shrunken old woman, and pry open my bedroom window. In my dreams, Bigfoot did just that. I woke before he could devour me.

When I was a little girl, my mother read tabloids, movie-star biographies, and murder mysteries by Agatha Christie and her various imitators. She left the mysteries on the end table in the living room, probably thinking that she didn't need to hide them from me. In theory, at nine or ten, I was too old to be scared by the cover illustrations and too young to be curious about the contents. And it was true that I didn't page through any of them, but not because I wasn't curious. I couldn't help staring at the paperbacks' covers, with their images of skeletons, houses in shadow, the occasional splotch of blood. One showed two long, skinny, disembodied arms with bony hands. Those arms came alive in a nightmare, a Hitchcock score shrieking as the hands reached for me.

When I was about eleven, my mother's diverticulitis flared, the pain so intense she sometimes had to go to the emergency room. Her doctors turned to invasive tests. By the time I was in my early teens, she had begun to explore true stories of extreme bodily torment. I can't see the timing as mere coincidence now that I've made the connection between my own crime obsession and my traumatic medical experiences.

A novelist's wildest inventions cannot shock or satisfy like the bizarre savagery of real-life violence. My mother chose the thrill and the dark glamour of the actual. True crime narratives turn charismatic murderers into celebrities. Where Liz Taylor and Grace Kelly, Mom's idols, needed extraordinary beauty and talent to win the world's attention, killers had only to be more prolific, more vicious, or more charming than their predecessors. Books about their exploits combined my mother's obsessions with fame and physical agony into one irresistible package.

Something I now understand very well.

Chapter 3

The Guy with the Knife

I n October 2006, three years before I started watching true crime TV, my medical adventures began.

That month, Andy and I took the elevator to the otolaryngology suite on the fourth floor of our local hospital. We stood for a moment, looking around and getting our bearings. Everything from the seat cushions to the walls to the wide curving desk was startlingly white, like heaven or a really expensive psychiatric facility.

This was not medicine as in flu shots and Pap smears and being urged to exercise more. This was capital-M Medicine. You were supposed to stand here and be awed.

We took seats in the waiting area, with its two rows of chairs upholstered in scratchy fabric. Andy sat as usual with his back straight but relaxed, the same way he stands, in the posture he has perfected over decades as a performing bluegrass musician. I curled into myself until I remembered not to and pulled my whole torso upright and rigid, until I forgot again and let my shoulders slide back into their familiar hunch.

The rows of chairs faced each other. Thyroid conditions

often afflict young women, but on this day, I was the only female patient under sixty-five. Andy and I were still new at this business of waiting for doctors, and still surprised each time we found ourselves surrounded by older folks, mainly women. There are two sides to Andy. The side I fell in love with is what the rest of the world sees: the articulate, graceful, guitar-strumming sweetheart. After six years, I knew the other side, too: the sarcastic grumbler with whom I can comfortably share my misanthropic thoughts. I'm your basic moody, introverted creative type, trying to make my way in rah-rah-keep-smiling America. In groups, I typically feel like the odd person out. Here in the waiting room, my relative youth made me downright alien. My hair was long and shiny, naturally black; my pale, bare skin unlined. Thanks to my height, five-eight, I looked like an Amazon among the elfin grandmas sitting all around me with their thin locks tormented by perms and dyes, splotches of blush and tanner on their deeply ridged faces. Occasionally, one of them caught my gaze and smiled, probably wondering what in the world I was doing here and wanting badly to tell me I should get a little sun.

Being younger than other patients by thirty years or more made me feel like some kind of *Ripley's* medical curiosity: Had my body started to invisibly decline, decades ahead of schedule?

A month before this visit, Andy had insisted I have a physical—my first in almost a decade. I was thirty-five, and I'd never gotten used to the idea that people with no discernible symptoms should sign up for the annual poke-and-prod. The only physicians I saw regularly were the psychiatrist who prescribed my antidepressants and the Planned Parenthood gynecologists who supplied me with birth control pills. When I was a kid, my mother only brought me to the pediatrician when I was sick with something she couldn't manage at home, which wasn't often.

Andy is a hypochondriac. He freely uses this term to describe himself, and I don't argue. When it comes to his own health, he imagines the worst, frequently viewing minor symptoms as signs of dread diseases. But his concern that I'd gone so long without a full checkup was hardly irrational. Vermont Medicaid had assigned me a new primary care provider, a nurse practitioner whose office was practically across the street from us. I had no excuse.

During the physical, the nurse practitioner found a nodule on my thyroid gland by palpating my neck. Tests followed. An ultrasound confirmed that there was indeed a gumball lodged in there. Next, a biopsy found atypical cells, which might or might not mean cancer. Ninety-five percent of solitary thyroid nodules were benign, I was told, but the only way to be certain was to remove it, along with the entire right half of the thyroid. The prospect of surgery scared me more than the possibility of cancer. I'd always been healthy. Of course I would fall into that 95-percent-benign category. Being one of the unlucky 5 percent seemed too exotic an outcome.

I did not then give depression its due as a serious illness. Even though I'd suffered from severe episodes since age fourteen; even though I'd attempted suicide in 1998, at twenty-seven. I'd kept my depression under control for the past three years with the help of medication, and I'd all but forgotten how dire it had been. *Always healthy*, I insisted, meaning always physically sound. I certainly never imagined I would develop multiple health conditions, like my mother. I believed I was fundamentally different from her, from my decision not to have children to my love of literature; except that I looked very much like her, and she, too, suffered from black moods.

And even if I'd counted depression as a serious illness— as I bloody well do now—I couldn't have claimed that it was unusual. There was nothing weird in my medical history. I'd broken my arm as a teenager; I'd had my share of colds and flus. How could I have cancer of the thyroid, a part of my body I'd never even thought about?

When the nurse finally called my name, "Mar-see-uh?" I didn't care about the mispronunciation. I was going in to meet my remaker.

The surgeon turned out to be a sixty-something man with a big grin and a grandfatherly air. I found myself warming to him.

"Yep, here it is," he said fondly, tapping a poster with his pen. The illustration featured a genderless humanoid with a dark-pink thyroid wrapped around the trachea, or windpipe, just below the Adam's apple.

From what I could see, the thyroid was nothing to be fond of. It was an ugly little thing with two lumpy, bumpy sides called lobes. The lobes clung desperately to either side of the trachea, as if they knew what was coming. They were connected in front of the trachea by a lumpy, bumpy bridge, the isthmus.

"Oh, yeah, there it is." I tried to look impressed.

He motioned for me to sit. I scrambled up onto the exam table in my street clothes. No going below the neck today, thankfully. Still, when he pressed his gloved fingertips against the base of my throat to examine the nodule, it was uncomfortably intimate.

There's a lot going on in and around the spot where the thyroid clings. It sits just below the larynx: it's hard to talk when somebody's palpating this area. This is where anxiety lives: the gagging, constricted sensation I was fighting now. Numerous blood vessels pass through the thyroid, and nerves critical to voice quality run close to the gland. Not to mention the major veins and arteries in the neck, and what we laypersons humbly call the windpipe, as if we pity ourselves for depending completely on something so slight.

Voice, fear, blood, and breath all intersect in the very spot where the surgeon was pressing.

I did not yet know about this complex network of vessels

and nerves. I'd just now learned the exact shape and position of the thyroid and the larynx from his creepy illustration.

"We'll make the incision right about here," he said, drawing his index finger lightly across my skin, just above the jugular notch, the visible hollow between the neck and the collarbones. I concentrated hard on not flinching. My heart rate spiked. "Now, I know you don't like that idea."

"You're young," he continued, "so you don't have wrinkles—*yet*." He grinned, and I forced a little laugh.

I didn't yet know that killer physicians appear with some frequency in true crime TV, though not often enough to qualify as a trope. But I did know they existed, from news stories, crime dramas, and possibly from my mother. I wasn't actually thinking of them the day I met my surgeon, but they must have been lurking in the recesses of my memory.

Most killer doctors are men, as are the majority of murderers.

It's worth noting that one meaning of the verb *doctor* is to tamper with something, using deception, while *nurse* has only positive, maternal connotations: to feed, care for, watch over. In the popular imagination, nurses are angels, while doctors are either saviors or villains. Distrust of physicians in this country dates back to the origins of the modern-day profession in the eighteenth and nineteenth centuries, when patients often died of medical treatments before they could succumb to disease.

It's not that I hate all doctors. I hate *certain* doctors. But I couldn't possibly hate Dr. Sixtysomething. He was an adorable, almost saintly old man who exuded calm. It was like having the Dalai Lama as my surgeon. When I uttered his name, clinical heads nodded reverently. He'd performed hundreds of thyroidectomies; for all I knew, he could have rows of jars filled with briny solution lining the walls of his rec room.

Still, knowing rationally that my doctor was not a murderer and actually trusting him with my life were two very different things. I thought of him not as the surgeon with the scalpel, but the guy with the knife.

"We make the cut where there's already a line in your skin, so that as you age, the skin sort of sags over the scar. Then it's less noticeable."

"Well," I said, in what I hoped was a wry, unfazed tone, "I guess *that'll* be something to look forward to."

My dry delivery hit its mark. Dr. Sixtysomething chuckled, and we continued discussing the procedure. The idea of wearing a sizable scar on my neck wasn't my biggest concern at that moment. I was more unnerved by the prospect of having my throat sliced open. But I wasn't about to let the doctor know that.

At this early stage, I was very much invested in being what I thought of as the good patient, the one who nods, smiles, appears grateful, asks questions but not too many. The good patient doesn't get upset over nothing. Here was my jolly-grandpa surgeon, his every word and gesture telling me that this was no big deal to him, therefore it should be no problem for me. The more questions I asked, the more frightened I would seem. Doctors didn't like nervous patients, I figured. They wanted patients who were confident in their ability to heal.

I came through that meeting knowing only that the right half of my thyroid would be excised and examined. During surgery, a pathologist would perform a frozen section: He'd flash-freeze slices of the half thyroid and peer at them under a microscope, while I lay anesthetized on the table, my throat still open. If he found malignant cells, they'd assume that cancer had spread throughout the entire gland, or that it might, and the surgeon would go back in and remove the left lobe. Otherwise, I'd be sewn up and brought back to the PACU, or post-anesthesia care unit.

I did not ask about the risks of the procedure, the process of recovery, or the particulars of follow-up care. I tried to keep smiling while he explained the slice-and-dice of the hapless little organ.

"Don't *worry!*" Dr. Sixtysomething said as I left, patting me on the arm. "Everything will go just fine."

Oh, no. Had my face betrayed me? I figured that in his mind, I had no reason to be afraid, no right to my fear. He must think I was overreacting. He performed this kind of surgery all the time. I didn't want to give him the erroneous impression that I didn't trust his skill. Or to let him know that I didn't trust him.

"Of course." I put on my most convincing grin. "I know it'll go fine."

I certainly didn't want to head into the OR thinking, *I've pissed off the guy with the knife.*

One of true crime's tropes is the detective's mantra, *Stabbing is personal.*

If you simply want to get rid of someone, you use a gun. You'll still make a blood-soaked mess, but if you like, you can stand back from the victim while you do it. Fire once, maybe two or three times if you're not a great shot, and it's all over.

Using a knife is intimate. You have to come in close. You have to spend time and effort. The more stab wounds the killer inflicts, the more "passion" he has for the victim. If the victim is female, the killer is probably a husband or lover, or perhaps a stalker. He wants her deader than dead, as if he's not simply trying to annihilate the victim but their entire relationship, real or imagined. A few well-placed incisions would do the job, but he can spend more rage making fifty cuts, still more if he makes a hundred. He wants to see her struggle, wants to hear her beg for her life. Or else he doesn't want to hear another word out of this woman ever again. He believes she has ruined his life with her actual or perceived rejection, her insistence on fighting for sole custody of their children, her refusal to tolerate his affairs, and so he silences her by cutting her throat.

Wherever the killer stabs or slices the victim, her blood splashes all over him.

The knife-wielding male partner and his female victim appear on every true crime program that doesn't specifically focus on some other type of relationship, from ID's *Forbidden: Dying for Love* to *Dateline* to *Forensic Files*. There are plenty of knife-wielding women attacking husbands, too, in all of these programs, but male offenders are far more plentiful.

I have never experienced violence at the hands of a partner, or any other male acquaintance. But at the time I met my surgeon, I was still afraid of the serial predator, the kind my mother told me about—and if she hadn't told me, I would have gotten the picture from news stories about Ted Bundy when I was a teen in the '80s. The killer who enjoys hurting and silencing women, who is like the murderous husband in that he desires the intimacy of the knife or manual strangulation. Statistically speaking, I was far more likely to be sexually assaulted or murdered by someone I knew, but it didn't *feel* more likely.

I only met with Dr. Sixtysomething once before the surgery, so I couldn't have said I knew him. He was still a stranger with a knife.

Some believe Jack the Ripper was a medical professional. In four of the five murders typically ascribed to him, the female victims' bodies were mutilated in a way that indicated the killer understood human anatomy. Several victims had missing uteruses. All five had their throats slit.

Hannibal Lecter was inspired by a real-life Mexican doctor, convicted murderer and suspected serial killer Alfredo Balli Trevino. He cut his lover's throat with a scalpel and dismembered his body. He was convicted of this crime, and was believed to have killed and dismembered others.

Some doctors kill family members, fitting neatly into one of the major tropes of true crime: the murdering spouse. Some doctors kill patients. A lot of them. There are enough cases of doctors and nurses who prey on patients to warrant the term

Medical Serial Killers (MSKs). Some modern-day doctors are believed to have racked up enormous body counts of patient-victims, sometimes enabled by administrators who refused to consider that healers might in fact be killers. The one who stands out most in my mind is Michael Swango.

His last name and the basics of his story—a murderous young doctor allowed to hop from one facility to the next—aren't connected to my binge-watching true crime TV; they seem to come from further back in my memory. I might have seen the interview he gave on *20/20,* or read about him in a newspaper when he was convicted in 2000. Or maybe my mother heard about him and passed on the details to me while I asked her not to. Though she mostly liked her doctors, these men were often unable to help her. The medications she was prescribed for diverticulitis and colitis failed to mitigate her symptoms. An air of dread hung over her like a dark gray aura whenever she went to the hospital for yet another invasive test.

The story of a killer physician would have spoken to her dread. I learned from my mother's experience to fear doctors, their tools, and their machines. Swango would have increased my fear.

Recently, I came across Swango when researching medical murderers online. Realizing that I'd already heard of him, I filled in the finer details of his strange story. In medical school, in the early '80s, Swango was called "Double-O Swango, Licensed to Kill" by fellow students who were appalled by his smirking attitude toward death. He asked dying patients about their experience of pain, and seemed to take pleasure in their agony. Despite his reputation, he went on to become a neurosurgery resident at Ohio State University Medical Center. He harmed patients by administering poisons, or overdoses of medications his patients were already taking.

When I met my surgeon, I wasn't consciously thinking of Swango, but he was there in some dark corner of my mind, stoking my fears. Since learning more about him, I'm now focused on him for complex, conflicting reasons. I am terrified of ever again becoming a patient on a ward, feeling helpless, filled with dread about the next invasive test or procedure. When I imagine the additional threat of someone like Swango, hired by unwary hospital administrators and left to roam the wards, making his deadly injections, my already considerable fear skyrockets. I've had so many needles sunk into my flesh that Swango with his syringes is an all-too-vivid image.

Fear is uncomfortable—and it's fascinating. It is our most basic, most powerful emotion. It was something that was thrust upon me, but it's mine now. If I heighten it by thinking of Swango, I can gain some measure of control. I want to fully inhabit my fear, explore it, and know it. I want to understand the workings of my mind.

Swango is also oddly comforting in that he satisfies the part of me that still insists on seeing doctors as criminals. He validates my outsized anxieties: *See? Some doctors really are killers.* Of course, knowing he's in prison for life without the possibility of parole is what allows me to use him for these purposes; I'll never actually encounter him. And the chances that I'll ever become the victim of any killer doctor are slim.

Wherever Swango worked, nurses reported that healthy patients tended to die for unexplained reasons whenever he was around, but their concerns were dismissed by hospital administrators. Finally, a group of nurses went straight to the prosecutor. An exhumation of five bodies failed to yield sufficient evidence against Swango. He continued to work in the medical field as a paramedic and was convicted of aggravated battery in 1985 for poisoning his coworkers.

After his release from prison, Swango was able to find employment as a medical technician in hospitals around the country. He even secured another residency. The fact that no one thoroughly checked his background horrifies me almost as much as his crimes. It's like the culture of denial in an alcoholic family, the unspoken rules I absorbed growing up: *Don't look too closely. Don't ask too many questions. You might not like what you learn.*

When I thought of the upcoming surgery, fear swelled my veins. My pulse rose. My throat closed in on itself.

Andy quietly managed his own fears about the surgery and the possibility of cancer. We never had the *What will we do if you have cancer?* conversation. We had an unspoken agreement that I was just going to get through the procedure first. We weren't going to freak out prematurely.

It was late at night that I cried. Too late to wake Andy. Nothing's ever scheduled for midnight, so that was when I wept into the sofa cushions: *They're going to find cancer, spread everywhere. I'll never come home. I'll die in a hospital bed. I'll die on the table.*

When the tears stopped, I found myself on my knees, praying to God and beseeching the universe, too, in the same whispered messages, asking to stay alive, ending with both "amen" and "namaste" just to cover all the bases.

In the light of day, I tried to contain my worries. I knew there would be a small risk of damage to the laryngeal nerves, which could cause temporary or in rare cases permanent voice changes. That simply would not happen. The surgeon wouldn't take my voice. Not permanently. He would have it during the operation, when I wouldn't know it. When a tube down my throat would direct my breath. I would be silenced, for a time, but then I would wake. Breathe. Speak.

It would be better not to know. Better to wake once it was all over.

Does the body remember the injury?
So what if it did? I would not.

Chapter 4

Like Some Maniac

I stayed carefully busy in the weeks before surgery. I was a temp for Burton Snowboards, preparing purchase orders. It's hard to think of a work environment in which I would have been more conspicuously out of place. Maybe the Starship *Enterprise*.

I am that rare creature, a native Vermonter who dislikes outdoor activities. I find them inexpressibly boring. I hate getting wet, or cold, or sweaty, or assailed by insects. I loathe the notion of gear, the putting on and the taking off of which only extends the miserable experience. I'd much rather read a book. I'd never seen a snowboard up close until my first day at Burton, when I found the entryway lined with mounted prototypes. They looked like giant tongues. It took me a minute to realize what the tongues were.

I showed up, did my work, and kept quiet about everything that mattered to me. I told no one I was a writer. I hardly mentioned Andy. I tried to be pleasant. I said *Good morning* and *Good night* and *Wow, it sure is warm/rainy/cold/indeterminate out there.* Whenever the supervisor stepped out, I overheard excited conversations about basketball, baseball, volleyball, the game Americans call soccer and the rest of the world calls football, the game Americans call football, and golf. The moment the supervisor returned, they stopped talking, and I again heard the furious clacking of keyboards.

I believed I was shamefully behind in life. In college, I was a psychology major with literary aspirations, intent on becoming a therapist-novelist, or maybe a therapist-poet. After a few years of working with the developmentally disabled and the psychiatrically challenged as an untrained, low-paid support person, I smothered what was left of my do-gooder intentions and took refuge in a master's program in writing. Now, the book of essays I'd started in grad school remained unfinished, my freelance editing business had barely begun, and my student loan and credit card debts were forcing me to play secretary.

I wasn't about to reveal my pathetic struggles or the news about my troublesome thyroid to my temporary colleagues: these very settled, ambitious twenty-five-year-olds, mostly men, all studying for their MBAs at night and already planning for retirement. If no one knew a thing about me, was I really there? My desk, wedged into a dimly lit corner between the wall and someone else's cubicle, suggested I wasn't.

I kept each little box in my day planner filled with details. *9 a.m., Pre-op phone interview; 10 a.m. to 4 p.m., Burton; Evening, editing, Carol, 2 hrs.* The ordinary starred reminders to *Pick up Rx refills, Call temp agency, Buy milk.* Everything was contained between those neat horizontal lines, as if the knife would not carve its own territory, as if the day planner and not my skin held my life.

Determined as I was to live my regular boring existence until the moment they wheeled me into the OR, I had to stop sometimes, to admit that something irregular and not-boring was about to happen. I approached my supervisor at Burton—a shy, stocky man about my age—rapping my knuckles gently on the metal frame of his cube until he looked up from his computer screen.

"I need to talk to you about a small change in my schedule."

"Sure. What's up?"

"I'm having surgery next week—not anything serious, but I need a few days off."

Startled by the mention of surgery, and by the fact that I was speaking to him at all, he nodded. "Oh, oh, OK." He didn't ask what I was going in for. Just the way I wanted it.

If no one from this realm of *Dude, what's the score?* knew the details about my upcoming operation, was it really happening? Not during the hours I sat in my corner, plugging numbers into cells.

Surgery prep remains a lovely memory.

Arrival in pre-op, six a.m. Sleepiness muffling my fear. Nurses fussing over me: A little nest made on a gurney, pillows behind my back and blankets tucked around legs left bare by the thin cotton gown. Sticky squares on my chest around heart and lungs, a blood pressure cuff squeezing my upper arm with authoritative love. Monitors beeping faithfully. An IV thrust into my hand, a moment of sting and the briefest flutter of panic, and then the beautiful, beautiful Valium.

Andy sat on a stool next to the gurney, clutching his black leather coat, trying not to get tangled in the pink-and-beige-polka-dot curtains that separated me from the next patient. Every so often, our eyes met, and he forced a small smile.

"It's all right," I murmured.

"I know. Of course it is," he said, looking away from the tubes, the screens, the IV. This space was the definition of not all right. I got the drug that made me forget what was at stake. He got a beeper and a time estimate that would turn out to be off by about an hour.

I was completely blissed out when they came for me.

"Ready to go?" a nurse chirped, lifting the metal bars on either side of the gurney and clicking them into place.

"I'm all right," I told Andy again. I thought I saw the beginnings of tears in his eyes.

He nodded, looked at the nurse, kissed me on the forehead, and ducked out. He could not cry in front of me.

They wheeled me out, and around, and up, and through. Flat on my back, I watched the fluorescent ceiling lights flash over me, just as they do on medical dramas that show the patient's point of view with jerky camera movements. The OR did not look like TV. There were twenty people, not five. Nurses, the anesthesiologist, surgical residents, their movements gracefully choreographed. Everything was tinfoil shiny in the white light, every head was covered in a ballooning blue cap, everyone was beaming as if this were Disney World and we were all going to have the most fun *ever*.

My last memory is the pink-scrubbed face of a young woman, asking me, "How we doing, Marcia? Need some more Valium? Are you cold?"

My mouth felt thick. "Fine. *Yes*. A little," I managed, and immediately more Valium shot through my veins, microwave-warmed blankets got piled on top of me. I felt supremely cared for, mothered like a treasured infant.

Then nothing. Nothing I needed to know about.

After many hours of watching true crime TV, I find that the beautiful murdered woman is so ubiquitous, she seems less like a cliché and more like an inevitability.

We hear much more about white female victims who are considered attractive because, as a society, we're just not interested in women of color or women we deem unattractive. They get murdered, too, but we're far less likely to learn about these crimes, far less likely to care if we do learn about them.

"Beautiful" is, of course, a relative term. True crime TV

elevates ordinary prettiness to singular loveliness partly through interviews with grieving relatives, who understandably emphasize their lost loved one's positive qualities. The camera lingers on her portrait, chosen by her family as the image they want to remember, the image they hope the world will remember. The photo was taken in a moment when she was presumably looking her very best, her face carefully made up and glowing with happiness on her prom night or wedding day.

When it's time to reveal the corpse, many true crime shows use pretty actresses to stand in for the dead. These women are often made more beautiful by their elegant passivity. Crime scene photos ruin this effect with the frank ugliness of twisted limbs and stab wounds; I believe this is why many true crime programs rely instead on recreations. An actress who plays a corpse portrays a woman who has surrendered completely, gracefully. She is the picture of femininity. She is silenced, her arms outstretched like a fallen ballerina's, her eyes demurely closed, her stilled body exquisite as a statue. She is lovelier without anger, opinions, ambitions, desires. She is Snow White in her glass coffin, Ophelia drowned in the river.

I wonder if I was beautiful in my anesthetized state, before the breathing tube and the blade across my throat.

In *Dead Girls*, cultural critic Alice Bolin explores the trope of the young female corpse in television dramas, noting that one message of what she calls "the Dead Girl Show" is that "the girl body is both a wellspring of and a target for sexual wickedness." I find this idea everywhere in true crime TV.

It's as if pretty women are specially designed to be prey. As if their beauty is too great a temptation for the rapist and murderer, leaving him unable to control his impulses. Promiscuous women and prostitutes are clearly meant to be seen as responsible for the crimes committed against them. But stories of lovely "innocent" victims subtly, and I think unintentionally, imply that even these women are partly to blame for the violence that befalls them. The unspoken message, conveyed by the emphasis on the victim's appearance and by the discussion of what she was doing in her last hours, is: *Walking the streets with that body, that face, she should have realized men would notice. She should have been more careful.* Women are expected to publicly display their attractiveness to men, in gyms and bars and even in the workplace, but they are also responsible for the consequences, including sexual harassment, sexual assault, and murder. The male perpetrator is, in a sense, the real victim, a slave to the monstrous desires aroused by irresistible females.

I'm guilty of focusing on beautiful murdered women, guilty of rating victims on a scale of prettiness informed by the fashion magazines I used to read. *She's OK, pretty enough, but this one looks like a model or an actress.* The loss seems greater when the victim was or could have been a professional beauty, the ultimate fulfillment of women's duty to display their sexual allure. Sometimes, I catch myself thinking how the professional beauty's culpability in her own death also seems greater: *She should have known better than to go off alone with that man. Just look at her.*

It didn't seem crazy to think I, too, could be killed by a predator when I was in my teens and twenties. Back then, I knew I wasn't model-pretty, but I was pretty enough to attract bad men. Much later, it seemed crazy *not* to fear such a fate when I began watching true crime shows, a few years after the surgeon made this first incision at my throat.

The pathologist's frozen section revealed no cancer. I was stitched up and sent to the PACU with the left lobe intact. Andy finally got the beep—later, he would tell me how worried he'd been, how the waiting room had filled with entire families, people coming and going, while he sat watching every minute click past on the wall clock overhead—and he accompanied me to the hospital room where I would spend the night under observation. I don't remember who told me I didn't have cancer, but

I remember the joy of that night, the unfamiliar sense of being blessed with extraordinary good fortune.

I went home the next day, surprised at how little pain I felt: a mild soreness around the incision, stiffness in the back of my neck from the way my head had been positioned during the procedure. But they'd given me Vicodin to take home, and I swallowed it as prescribed, even though I didn't need it. I wanted that glorious hospital feeling back. To live once more in the familiar rooms of our modest rented condo but filtering it all through the godlike vision granted by narcotics: the kitchen, its old humming refrigerator and basket of teas and spices on the countertop; long, open living room with my tall bookshelves, Andy's guitar case, our sagging beige hand-me-down sofa, the rose-colored area rug with its abstract black-and-brown splatter design, and the sliding-glass-door view of marshy woods; upstairs, our minimally furnished bedroom, bathroom, and my office, silver laptop and stacks of client files on my yard-sale desk.

Oh, Andy and work, love and comfort, I have everything, everything.

"I'm just glad you're home," Andy kept saying, as if there were anything left to worry about.

Silly love, of course I'm home. They didn't find any cancer.

Three days after the surgery, the Vicodin used up, I stood in front of the upstairs bathroom mirror. My godlike powers were gone, and I was tired. My long black hair always made my pale skin look paler, and today I appeared ghastly. It was time to remove the dressing, according to my discharge directions. Deep breath; shut the door. I began to peel off the long, wrinkled strip of clear adhesive that resembled packing tape. I let the white gauze bandage fall with it.

"Oh, no," I said out loud. "Oh, fuck."

The incision, the one I told myself I didn't care about, was longer and more raised than I'd imagined: a three-and-a-half-inch Frankenstein pucker. It underscored my chin like the mark of a middle school English teacher's angry red pen. A piece of blue nylon thread held it together, giving it a slightly jagged appearance.

Now it was Andy's turn to remain calm while I got upset. I went out and pulled him into the bathroom so he could see it under the light.

"It looks *awful*," I moaned.

"Oh, honey, no, it doesn't." He gazed at it admiringly, as though it were a marvelous feat of cosmetic surgery, as though some doctor-artist had made my cleft lip disappear. "Wow. Would you look at that?"

"I *am*. It's horrible."

"No, no. It's incredible, really. It hardly looks like anything happened."

Are you kidding? Are you blind? *It's like some maniac went after me with a carving knife.*

I kept my impressions of violence to myself. I didn't want to take away Andy's wonderment, his joy over things turning out right.

In true crime TV, the complexities of a woman's self are erased by her murder. Her entire existence is reduced to sentimental labels: good daughter, always-smiling coworker or student, devoted mother, loving wife. In death as in life, women only matter in terms of their relationships to others.

The murdered woman's consciousness is gone, and we never learn what it contained. Unless she was involved in "bad" behavior that led directly to her death, like having an affair or abusing drugs or working in the sex trade, we learn nothing of her psychological makeup. We are only hearing her name and seeing her beaming face in high school yearbooks or wedding photos because she was murdered. That is the source of this sliver of fame we allow her. That is why we will tolerate the tearful recollections of her mother, her sister, her best friend, for a few seconds each if the show is a half hour long, for a minute or so in hour-long programs.

The killer's psychology is what counts, especially if he was a stranger to the victim, and most of all if he is believed to be a serial offender. His childhood scars, his relationship with his mother, his dating history, his IQ—these details interest us. Women are supposed to be silent, anyway. What the culture tries to do every day, a little at a time, the killer accomplishes in minutes with a rope, a knife, his bare hands. He takes her voice forever. It is his confession or obfuscation we listen to with rapt attention, his words that are carefully preserved by investigators for the trial that will prove just how important he is.

He is a master at what he does. Her body is his evidence. He takes away her beauty as my highly skilled surgeon took away mine.

When I looked at my scar, I knew there was something more than vanity at stake. Where was the healthy young woman I believed I'd always been? Who was this scarred, scared figure in the mirror? I had come through surgery just fine; I didn't have cancer. Yet I looked like a sick person.

Worse, I looked like something dire had happened to me. The sight of my incision filled me with shame that I interpreted as simple embarrassment.

I knew what to do: hide.

The weekend before I returned to Burton, I bought a silk scarf, in a muted shade of plum. I never wore scarves. Facing that bathroom mirror I had come to dread, I wound the slippery fabric several times around my neck, and voilà! The incision disappeared, and my previous self, Healthy Young Woman, returned. She smiled at me in the mirror. *There.* Now *it looks like nothing happened.*

"Awesome scarf!" women commented on my first day back

at work. I thanked them for their compliments, pretending that this was just a fashion choice.

That day, I learned that my temp assignment was coming to an end. It was Monday. Wednesday of the following week, the day before Thanksgiving, would be my last day at Burton.

If I could have hidden behind my desk in the corner, I might have made it through my final days in better shape. But long hallways separated Purchasing from the bathroom, the vending machines, and the building's entrance. If I wanted a 3 Musketeers pick-me-up or my usual swift getaway at exactly four o'clock, I had to make the trek. The relentless, empty-headed cheer of the company's youth-worship culture had merely been annoying before the surgery. Now it took a bite out of my ass. The serious guys in Purchasing were still OK by me, but the other twentysomethings made me nuts. I cringed at the shrill chatter of young women in the break room:

"Omigod! *Awe*some! Super cute! Europe? No *way!*"

And the creepy drawl of slouching young men: "S'up. Dude? Sweet. Y'know, whatever, 's all good, yo?"

Anger rushed up so fast it frightened me. I wanted to smash the empty coffee urns against their skulls. For making me feel not-young in a final way. For sounding happy, carefree. Wanting fun instead of craving safety. For the days they never spent in hospitals.

Of course, I had no way of knowing whether they'd ever been sick. Some might have struggled with asthma since childhood. Some might have had cancer.

All I could see was their unmarred skin. Their beauty and their lives intact. My incision spoke of death, even though I wasn't dying. It would remind me every day of my mortality.

And back then I couldn't have put words to the rest, but I see now that the incision also spoke of my consent to being marked by a man—violently and permanently. I had little choice but to agree to the surgery, but I believe that on an unconscious level, I had the sense I should have protected myself. This was the source of the shame I felt when I looked in the mirror. The incision revealed that my beauty was cut away as I lay on the table like a corpse, for I had also allowed myself to be rendered passive. Now I was ugly, of less worth than if I had actually been killed. What was a woman's life worth without beauty? Had I died, my unmarred skin would have lived on in photographs, in people's memories, the way murdered women's beauty survived them.

The day after I learned my assignment at Burton was coming to an end, eight days after the surgery, I returned to the hospital for a follow-up visit with Dr. Sixtysomething. To contain my nervousness around him, I compartmentalized: Today, he wasn't the guy with the knife. He wasn't a surgeon, just a physician who was going to take out my sutures quickly and painlessly, as the process had been described to me. And how silly it was that I ever thought of the incision as the mark of a maniac. Clearly *I* was the crazy one.

When he entered the exam room, I saw that his usual impish grin was gone, and I knew.

He asked how I was feeling. "Great," I said.

He snipped the end of the blue nylon thread and pulled it out of the incision. No pain, as advertised.

"That was easy," I said, hoping against hope to bring that grin back to his face.

He looked at me. "Marcia, I'm sorry ..."

He explained that the pathologist had reexamined the excised half of my thyroid, after I was sewn up. What wasn't readily visible in the first inspection became apparent in the second. I hadn't known there would be a second look. I had thought no cancer meant no cancer.

He wrote down the details for me on a prescription-pad-sized piece of paper, which I still have. A small space, as if he thought he could contain the impact of the news: *Papillary carcinoma, 2 cm., follicular variant.* Stage I, he called it.

This type of thyroid cancer at this stage was 98 to 99 percent treatable, the doctor said. He would need to reopen my still-healing incision and take out the remaining left half of my thyroid; it might also contain cancer cells, too small for tests to detect. Five to six weeks after the second operation, I would return to the hospital as an outpatient for a dose of radioactive iodine. Thyroid tissue absorbs iodine. Any particles of tissue too tiny to be removed surgically, and any metastases beyond the gland, would be destroyed.

Dr. Sixtysomething's face was a study in sorrow and regret, though he had not made a mistake. Later, when I read the pathology report, it didn't sound as if the pathologist had made a mistake, either. The cancer had been difficult to detect, in what must have been a strictly limited time frame, since I was still on the operating table while he examined the frozen section. Dr. Sixtysomething had all those decades of experience, all the skill a patient could possibly ask for. But he couldn't prevent cancer. All he could do was carve it out when he found it. He was my surgeon again, but he was also a man diminished. His breezy discussion of surgery at our first appointment felt distant now. He did not want to cut me again.

"Every so often, I have to give this kind of news to a young person," he said. I realized how he must have dreaded this visit.

"Don't worry," he told me before we parted. "The second procedure will go fine." I was still too stunned to evaluate this prediction. I just nodded. Dazed, I left the exam room and found myself at the checkout desk. The usually smiling scheduler looked grim. Next surgery: two weeks.

How do I tell Andy?

In the waiting room, I began, "Honey—" and couldn't continue.

"I know," Andy said softly. "You were in there so long, I figured it out."

I held it together until we reached a bench in the hallway, where I sank into Andy's arms, weeping. A storm of emotions hit me: shock over the diagnosis, relief that it wasn't something worse, grief for that always-healthy self who now seemed gone for good.

I float over this scene of the two of us, alone in the vastness of the hospital, enclosed in a small, airless pocket of fear. I want to tell this couple that everything's going to be OK. And not OK. And then OK again. I want to tell them they'll be able to handle what they can't yet understand, what they don't know lies ahead. But even if that were possible, I couldn't do it. I couldn't bring myself to tell them this is only the beginning.

Chapter 5

Bodies

When I was very little, I used to sit on my father's lap. At some point, I stopped. Long before you would think I needed to.

I am sure I loved my father when I was a small child. I don't remember what that love felt like. I didn't know what his drinking meant; I only knew the icy-burn scent of cheap vodka, a smell that came from his skin, as did the smell of cigarettes, that odor of intentional decay.

My mother did not permit me to enjoy the few years little girls have to see their fathers as heroes. She enumerated all of his faults to my teenaged sisters, as usual not thinking that I was listening. I didn't understand all that his failings meant, but I absorbed the list: inattentive husband, half-assed parent, reckless money manager. In those days, his drinking seemed the least of her concerns.

I felt the danger he posed to us: the house he might again bring down around our heads because he'd spent the mortgage payments on gardening supplies, liquor, poker; the hand he might raise in anger if our early spankings were forgotten. I didn't understand why he would put us at risk, why he wouldn't make my mother happy.

One night, when I was about eight and well past the lap-sitting phase, I was watching TV alone with my father. The basement family room, its tiny windows eye-level with the lawn, was always dim, even in the middle of the day. It adjoined the bedroom my father had built for my sisters. He had nailed real barn board onto the walls of the family room. Mom had knelt for hours stroking deep brown paint onto the cement floor, then laid down a store-bought, rust-and-cream braided rug that ran the length of the room. But nothing could disguise the fact that this was the basement, the damp space that yawned beneath us. The worn brown-and-rust-tweed couch smelled dank. My father's green quilt-patterned recliner stank of old cigarette smoke and little spills of vodka. There were no backs on the stairs; at least Mom had tacked ribbed plastic protectors onto each step. Climbing those stairs always scared me. I imagined monsters grabbing my feet. I saw myself falling backward into empty space.

At that age, I was not yet able to tell how drunk either parent was, unless the impairment was severe. While my father stayed seated in his recliner, grunting occasionally with laughter over *The Dukes of Hazzard* or the antics of wild elephants on *Mutual of Omaha's Wild Kingdom*, he didn't seem drunk, despite the ever present cans of beer and juice glasses filled to the brim with vodka. I didn't count them, didn't know to count them, didn't know how many drinks were too many. We were just spending time together, not because we'd sought out each other's company but because Mom wanted to watch her own shows upstairs.

I was embarrassed and confused when Daisy Duke paraded around in front of her cousins, Luke and Bo, and Uncle Jesse, wearing her signature skintight cutoff shorts. I didn't understand why she wasn't ashamed to look like that in front of her male relatives, or why she wanted other men to stare and whistle at her. Otherwise, I thought the show was funny.

My father never commented to me about Daisy Duke. He and I mostly viewed our programs in easy silence. But I knew there might come a point in the evening when he would require Mom's assistance to stand, to safely climb the stairs and make it to the bathroom and the bed. I knew to be gone well before she appeared, glowering at him: "I suppose you need help, don't you?"

On this particular night, he was ready to come upstairs earlier than expected.

He lost his balance as he tried to stand from the recliner, and fell on top of me where I sat on the couch, bracing himself with shaking arms on either side of my body. His startled face loomed before mine, eyes wide, as if he didn't recognize me. I don't remember if I cried out, don't remember Mom coming to pull him upright and walk or drag him toward the stairs. She must have come because he did make it across the room and up the stairs, and could not have done so by himself without falling again. I must have scampered upstairs ahead of them.

That night, with my father deposited in bed on the other side of my bedroom wall, I couldn't sleep. I didn't know what I feared, exactly. Mom sat on the edge of my bed, which was rare. She had probably heard me crying.

"Is he going to come in here?" I asked her.

"Of course not. He's not going to come in here," she scolded, softly.

She did not look at me. She knew I was asking about something I couldn't yet imagine.

One night, when I was eleven, I dressed for bed in a short, robin's-egg-blue nightshirt, styled like a football jersey, with white numerals stitched on the front. Thin, clingy material, the kind that comes out of the dryer crackling with static. One of my sisters had tired of it, and given it to me. How I would regret wearing it that night.

We were watching TV in the family room, with its dark corners and spiky shadows. I was curled up next to my sister on the old, worn sofa, its rough brown fabric scratching my bare legs. Mom and my sister whispered something to each other, laughing. Something about the numbers on my jersey.

My father was sitting right there between the sofa and Mom's armchair. Vodka bottle on the brown-painted concrete floor next to his recliner.

I looked down at the numbers on my chest, to see what was so funny.

I heard my father say Mom and my sister were talking about my breasts. I heard my father name my breasts with animal words, like he was eyeing a swollen cow needing to be milked.

"Dad!" Mom admonished him gently, laughing harder.

He did not touch me. He never would. He didn't have to. His words were greasy fingers, groping me, tearing off that thin sheath so they could all see this new flesh that was not yet mine.

I shrank, hunching my shoulders, making my chest concave. I couldn't speak.

That moment was a knife. It was exactly then that my childhood ended, cut away cleanly with a single stroke. Before that moment, I was just a girl. After, I was a creature, a stupid girl-woman beast rendered voiceless. I was a joke, the canned laughter bursting live from my father and mother and sister.

The next time, still when I was just eleven, he towered over me as I sat on the living-room floor. Unsteady, drink in hand, he stared down. And laughed. He was watching my body becoming something else, he said. It was exciting, and somehow hilarious at the same time. I would get bigger, and bigger still. I understood that he was going to keep watching me. I was like something growing in his vegetable garden, flesh swelling on a stalk. He did not speak of harvest, but any growing thing knows it can be taken the day it is deemed ready.

Mom was there, too. Maybe my sisters. Maybe they all laughed. He was so tall, weaving, and the room was dim, yet somehow there was enough light for him to see me. He blotted out the rest of the world. Except my mother. I don't remember if she admonished him again, not that it would have made any difference. He wasn't going to stop. Not that night. Not until I grew up and away from him.

I did not want to live inside this flesh that crawled with dirt and fear. I wept for my child's body, wept that I could never live there again.

What was I now? I was nothing more than these small, fat rounds of flesh bound in the elastic of the training bra that left red welts. Wrapped and presented like a gift: here she is. Small, the world agreed, too small to make men want me. I knew this from TV and Mom's celebrity tabloids. I knew this from Mom. Flat, she lamented, as if I had failed her. As if I were her failure. Her disappointing body passed on to me. My sisters pointed, whispered, and laughed. It was cute. I was growing up. But they knew the world. Flat, they agreed.

I didn't understand. Why was I supposed to be a woman men wanted if I was still a girl? I had to stay a virgin or else be a slut. I wanted to be a virgin for a long, long time, but in the meantime, I wanted a boyfriend. Just chaste hand-holding on the playground, notes with scribbled hearts passed in class, maybe a kiss. But boys weren't interested in me. If boys were not yet men, why did breasts matter to them? Wasn't it enough to be pretty? Was I pretty? Why did my breasts make me woman enough for my father and no one else?

I wanted to cut them off.

True crime TV gives the distinct impression that America is a sexually treacherous place for girls of all ages. Judging from statistics and the disclosures of the #MeToo movement, it is no exaggeration. It doesn't take many hours of watching true crime to amass a host of horrifying stories: Prepubescent girls abducted at knifepoint from their bedrooms. Teenage girls who disappear on their way to school. Women in prison who describe being molested by their brothers, uncles, fathers.

When the twentieth anniversary of JonBenet Ramsey's 1996 murder approached, networks from CBS to A&E to ID flooded television airwaves with documentaries about the case. The unsolved killing of a beautiful girl still captivated viewers, including me.

I watched several of the documentaries. There were the infamous pageant videos that so shocked and fascinated the public when they were first aired after the murder, showing JonBenet heavily made up, extravagantly coiffed, and often wearing costumes that look much too adult, including a Vegas showgirl-style ensemble and an off-the-shoulder dress paired with black nylons. Then there were photos of JonBenet I'd never seen before: candid shots taken by her family, in which she appears without makeup or cascades of curls. And there were autopsy photos, which thankfully do not show her face—hers is one dead face I don't want to see—but do show the garrote around her neck and strands of blonde hair.

I watched the 2016 documentaries in the same place where I do all of my true crime viewing, in my living room. I realized that all of this time, I had viewed JonBenet as a little woman, not a little girl. The only images of her I'd ever seen were the pageant videos and accompanying portraits. I'd bought into the sexualized façade.

Standing in stark contrast to the videos, the candid photos show a sweet six-year-old looking six. These shots and those of the garrote and the strands of hair brought home for me the horror of this child's murder.

John and Patsy Ramsey were formally exonerated after twelve years as suspects in JonBenet's murder. I don't believe the Ramseys killed their child. I cannot imagine the depths of their grief. Yet I do find them guilty of teaching their very young daughter that her worth lay primarily in her beauty, and of contributing to the wider culture of early sexualization that damages all girls. Someone who also viewed JonBenet as a little woman, who may or may not have seen her in her pageant costumes but who probably found validation for his appetites in countless media images of girls made to look like women, must have entered her house that night.

I am still fascinated by the pageant videos, seduced all over again by her hyperfeminine appearance. JonBenet sometimes looks as if she's having fun and sometimes seems tentative, making me wonder if her mother, a former pageant contestant, ever pushed her to compete. The videos allow me to explore what happened to me at eleven, when I was made a woman much too soon; I know my experience is the main source of my fascination. The videos also allow me to minimize what happened to me, as if being sexualized at eleven doesn't matter because many girls are sexualized much younger. They make me ashamed to watch, ashamed to know I'm captivated by her beauty. They make me angry at her parents, at my parents. JonBenet's mother surely thought she was merely introducing her daughter to an activity she herself had enjoyed. My father surely thought he was joking when he commented on my body, to the extent that he thought about what he was doing at all.

More than a decade later, a psychiatric nurse practitioner would give a name to the three years of low moods that began at eleven: dysthymia, a chronic, typically less severe form of depression. The dysthymia and my first episode of major depression at

fourteen would go undiagnosed until then. I told the nurse practitioner when, but not how, my consuming sadness began. He
only wanted symptoms, past and present. I was there for meds,
not therapy.

So, you were eleven, twelve, thirteen? Ah, puberty. Of
course. He took his notes. Took me down. Did not ask what
happened. So, full-blown depression by fourteen? Teenaged girl,
mood disturbance, uh-huh, got it.

As if being a girl were an illness born purely of biology.

I may have inherited a predisposition to depression from my
parents, but my illness was born of injury. It emerged when my
childhood was severed. When my body was stripped, dirtied,
made sick with fear in its very cells. My father accomplished all
of this with leers, slurred jokes. Only words. Only words turning
flesh to dread.

The summer I was fourteen, there were the hot, still, late nights
at home.

The drunkwalks were by now almost nightly events. My
parents crashed in their separate beds at the opposite end of the
hall, the bathroom between them and me. How many times did
I dare myself to move softly from my bedroom to the bathroom,
soundlessly slide open the mirrored door of the medicine cabinet? Many more times than I'd be comfortable with if I had a
daughter.

Those nights are why I don't have a daughter.

I've never been able to imagine being a house when for most
of my life I have considered ways to tear this house down.

I was too afraid to run away from home. I was too tired
to run away from home. A woman's body drew attention from
men. A woman's body was a fearsome weight for a girl.

There was only one way to truly go missing.

The full bottle of extra-strength Tylenol in the medicine
cabinet. The cyanide poisonings of 1982 had fixed Tylenol in

my mind as a means of death. Though the poisonings stopped after the introduction of tamper-resistant packaging, Tylenol still seemed dangerous. One hundred tablets. A chalky mound in my belly.

It never occurred to me that it might not be enough to free me from my woman's body forever.

The medicine cabinet was also cluttered with my mother's medications. I didn't know what they were, couldn't pronounce the names. I only knew they were meant to assuage the savage pain in her intestines. They all failed her.

I didn't know if those mysterious potions would kill me. Tylenol was familiar. I sometimes took it for the occasional headache, tapping out exactly two tablets into my palm, afraid to take more than the recommended dosage.

On those hot, late nights, I took no Tylenol at all. I hadn't quite given up on life. Not yet.

Death would remain a powerful fantasy, the ultimate solution to the problem of living in a vulnerable female body. Contemplating suicide so young changed me forever. I will always see death as the route to absolute safety, to perfect rest. I think there must be women with histories of depression and trauma who watch true crime in part because they see death the same way. In viewing real crime scene photos, I sometimes forget the suffering that led to the brutal end, and focus on the fact that nothing and no one can ever harm this woman again.

I would not leave that house for another four years.

Silence was my rebellion: I enacted an estrangement from my father while still living under his roof. I would talk to him less and less until I stopped altogether except for the occasional forced monosyllable. When I heard the crunch of gravel in the driveway each afternoon, I gathered my books from the living-room sofa and went to my room. My mother said nothing, only rose from the recliner so that my father could take his rightful place there when he entered.

Later, he took his place at the head of the dinner table; I sat to his left, not looking at him, talking a little to my mother, who sat to his right. My separation was part fury, part self-preservation. When I had to be in my father's presence, I thought that speaking to him would draw his eyes to me, elicit more greasy remarks.

My silence and my hiding did protect me. He made few comments about my body after I minimized his opportunities to do so.

I still have trouble sleeping; I wake up ablaze with alarm. Perhaps I think I went to sleep in my own house and woke up in 1985. Depression is a tunnel inside me that opens onto that teenage bedroom.

Chapter 6

Killers and Motives

One afternoon, shortly before the end of my temp assignment, I was eating lunch at Burton, away from the din of the break room. Through sheet glass windows, I looked out over endless banks of white clouds, with a layer of blue underneath. Heaven blue. A potent slant of sun reached me after many days of gray.

The sky was this shade of blue on a July morning, eight years before the cancer, when I gave up fighting the most savage depressive episode I've ever had. I was in utter despair after the failure of a tumultuous five-year relationship, unable to imagine a future in which I would not be alone. I desperately wanted a career as a writer, but couldn't imagine summoning the courage to pursue one. I was convinced my life would not improve, that my existence was a mistake. For weeks, I had obsessed day and night over the idea of killing myself with pills. After composing a brief, apologetic note addressed to friends and family, I took an overdose of a prescription drug and climbed under the covers on my futon, waiting to die. My roommate slept at the opposite end of the apartment. With my bedroom door firmly shut, I figured that if she woke early and passed by on her way to the kitchen, she'd assume I was still asleep, and wouldn't interrupt me.

My state of mind was such that I was convinced I would be welcomed into the golden light of heaven by Jesus. The gentle yellow of the sun, so high above my little bedroom window, would envelop me completely. (Jesus? Never before or since have I thought of Jesus as anything other than an ordinary guy. And heaven? Seems way too wonderful to be real.)

An hour later, I realized I was growing sleepy and roused myself. Suddenly, I was afraid to die, though I didn't quite want to live either. I had no idea what this drug might do to me before it killed me. I imagined convulsions, constricted breathing, stabbing abdominal pain. All I'd wanted was to peacefully drift away. If it hadn't happened by now, perhaps what lay in store for me instead was torment.

I emerged from my bedroom and confessed to my roommate, who had just awakened, and who was so horrified she couldn't look at me. She called for an ambulance. I went to the ER in the same hospital where I would later be treated for cancer.

Gastric lavage felt like a fitting punishment for a suicide attempt. A nurse shoved a large tube down my throat while two others held me down on the gurney. It didn't feel like they were saving my life. It felt like they were choking me to death. The nurse with the tube locked eyes with me as I struggled to get away. "Marcia. *Marcia*. We have to do this. You have to let us do this."

I understood. I grew still. I let them do it. Water in. Water out. Finish with charcoal to absorb what hadn't been washed up.

A few days later, I was riding along the highway in a friend's car, rolling fast into the sunset. Strapped into the passenger seat, I felt myself hurtling toward the light I thought I'd have to die to get to. I saw that it was the light of the living. I didn't know what to do except take it in. I was still afraid of being the hapless passenger, speeding in a direction she did not choose. But I was beginning to want life again, and the brilliance opening before me indicated that life wanted me. My existence was not a mistake. The yellow sun wasn't dying; it was beckoning before it sank to its night's rest. Streaking my face in gold, it told me it was all right to rest for a time, then rise slowly to my rightful place.

I never would have imagined that a few months after my overdose, I would enter a prestigious graduate program in writing. Or that a year after the overdose, I would meet the love of my life.

How strange all these years later, to hear the words *papillary carcinoma* and think fiercely, *I will live.* As if my desire to remain on earth had never wavered.

When Andy and I met, he was thirty-six, and I was a scattered but no longer depressed twenty-eight-year-old. I was working in the book department of a Borders store in Burlington when I noticed a cute guy with molasses-brown eyes, a new hire in the music department. Andy, unassuming in all things, wore no product in his curly brown hair, unusual in 1999, and dressed in casual button-up shirts tucked into the waistband of his jeans. Still in my wannabe New Yorker phase, I frequently dressed all in black. I was dating someone who wouldn't call me his girlfriend, so I had my eyes open.

During our first break-room conversation, I made sure Andy knew I was studying writing in an MFA program. I made sure every human being I met knew I was in an MFA program. Andy was one of the few people who said, "Oh, really?" with genuine interest.

"I write songs," he told me, then hesitated. "I'm a bluegrass guitarist," he finally added.

I blinked. The guitarist part sounded good. "Bluegrass. Is that like country?"

He smiled. "Sort of. You know the theme song to *The Beverly Hillbillies?*"

"Sure." The show was a childhood favorite.

"Then you know what bluegrass is."

"Oh! I never knew what ... *that* was."

I would later learn that this was Andy's style as a private music teacher: to make people comfortable, to tell them they knew more than they thought they knew. I would also learn that he was as interested in me from that first interaction as I was in him, but he was worried I might be a smoker, being a black-clad writer and all. That would have been a deal-breaker.

A few months after this encounter, he approached me again in the break room as we were preparing to leave for the night. Taller than me by several inches, he bent forward a little and spoke in a low voice.

"I don't mean to put you on the spot or anything, but I was wondering if you were seeing anyone?" I was impressed that he thought he might be making me uncomfortable; no guy had ever expressed such a concern when asking me out. I had no idea how nervous he was.

"I would—but actually, I'm seeing someone." Meaning I would have gone out with him if not for the not-quite-a-boy-friend. I felt I had to be honest. Andy seemed like someone who deserved and expected honesty.

"Oh. Oh, all right." He clutched his brown leather jacket and quickly walked away.

In the weeks that followed, we were self-conscious around each other. Meanwhile, things weren't going so well with the not-boyfriend. He was also a musician, and much more inter-ested in composing moody New Age pieces on the elaborate set of keyboards in his living room than in taking me out for din-ners and movies. Had I lost my chance with Andy? I ultimately decided to find out. In a rush of what I thought of as courage, I fired the not-boyfriend over the phone; he wasn't especially upset. Then I waited ten minutes, which seemed an appropriate length of time, and called Andy.

"I thought you might like to know that I've broken up with the guy I was seeing." I didn't tell him just how recently.

"I have to say, I'm not sorry to hear that," Andy replied.

We agreed to meet for drinks at a quiet restaurant after our shifts the next night. Still feeling courageous, I dressed in a hot-pink-and-orange shirt for the occasion, although I stuck with black pants. I got out of work before he did, and brought along a volume of *The Best American Poetry*, both to remind him of the writing-student thing and to have something to focus on while I waited in the restaurant. I was so nervous I didn't absorb a single line. Still, Andy says that when he showed up that night, I looked up coolly from the book and said, "Oh, hi," as if I'd forgotten he was coming.

Andy had a beer. I ordered a chardonnay, which I thought would impress him; it didn't. We talked about the guitar students he taught at his apartment, my studies (of course), how we'd both been raised in Vermont, and how Borders was OK as far as retail jobs went. We both hinted at not being close to our families. At the end of the evening, he walked me home, and instead of kissing me, he shook my hand. I felt both excited and secure, a combination I'd never experienced on a first date, or any date. It was as if he already cherished me, and was being extra careful not to screw this up.

In true crime TV, relationships tend to be super serious from the beginning. The phenomenon of love at first sight, the whirlwind courtship that leads to an engagement in months or weeks, the unceremonious dumping of an unsatisfactory partner in favor of the just-met dreamboat—these clichés play out over and over, usually ending in disaster. The quick-to-propose boyfriend sometimes becomes the killer husband: the recklessness that has him leaping into marriage is the same recklessness that drives him to violence.

Andy and I were powerfully attracted at first sight, and fell in love quickly. My dispensing of the not-boyfriend was one of the few times in my life when acting on impulse was the right move. But Andy's steadiness saved us, I think. He was careful not to rush an already intense, rapidly evolving process. I intuited that if I asked for too much, too soon, he would balk. If he hadn't shaken my hand at the end of our first date, signaling that he considered the date over, I would have invited him up. If we didn't both have roommates, I probably would have suggested we live together almost immediately. Pushing for intimacy was how I approached previous relationships, and they had all ended badly, though never with the threat of bodily harm. I sensed that Andy was protecting me from getting hurt, as much as he was protecting himself.

The binary star is actually a pair of stars that depend on each other's gravitation to stay in orbit.

After six years together, Andy and I were a two-star system. No kids, superficial friendships. We were both introspective worrywarts, the truth-telling youngest children in our troubled families. Being the truth-teller had strained Andy's difficult relationships with his mother and brother to the point of near estrangement.

I, too, had grown up as an outsider in my family. My siblings were ensconced in what passes for suburbia in Vermont, with well-kept homes, sensible careers, SUVs, and exactly two children each. They loved me and I loved them, a kind of genetic default setting. But how does one love a stranger? Awkwardly. With effort. We all lived within twenty miles of each other. They got together frequently, but I didn't see them often.

So Andy and I viewed problems as things we had to solve on our own. After all, no one could possibly understand us the way we understood each other. A powerful force kept us together, a combination of love, admiration, and dependence.

By now, we had been through—we thought—everything: I cranked out the thesis for my master's, graduating just before we celebrated our first anniversary. Three years in, I had lost both parents, my father's death compounding my grief over my mother's. Andy's father died a year after mine. Andy had seen me through two severe bouts of clinical depression. We scraped by on income from retail and temp jobs, supplemented by Andy's music students and gigs, and my slowly growing roster of editing clients.

We were together: monogamous, splitting the bills. But not married.

I'd wanted to marry Andy since we first declared our love for each other, barely a month into our relationship. It was then he told me flat out he didn't want children; he was nervous but resolute. I told him I didn't want children, either. In reality, I didn't know for certain, but I knew I wanted Andy, and I knew that if I told him I might want kids one day, he'd walk away, preferring to lose me after a few weeks rather than after a few years, my biological clock wired to a relationship-detonation bomb. We didn't talk about marriage. Not then. In time, we would marry, I was sure. Clearly, Andy had brought up the kid issue because he was already thinking long-term. One day, he would propose.

Five years into our relationship, when after many moves we had finally landed in a place we could call home, a quiet condo in South Burlington with below-market rent, I began pressing the marriage issue. By then I was thirty-four, and I'd more or less settled into the idea that I would never be a mother. It wasn't that I didn't want a child at all. It was that I didn't want one *enough*, and certainly not enough to tear down my relationship with Andy, whose position on fatherhood had never wavered. After all of our challenges, I longed for a peaceful, stable existence together. I wanted us to focus on each other.

What I desired seemed simple to me: a definition of our relationship that we could make public. Friends and even acquaintances were asking when—not if—we were going to get hitched, take the plunge, or whatever awful image of entrapment or drowning they used for matrimony. I kept making my case, several times a year, every year. As if reason and repetition could sway him.

"I don't want the label, 'husband,'" he said when I first brought up marriage. He'd been divorced in his mid-twenties. "I'm tired of being told who I am. I don't want people to think they know who we are just because we're married. If anyone wants to know the story of us, I'll be glad to sit them down and tell them. That's what I want: to be able to tell the story. Not have it told for me."

"I love the word 'husband.' I want you to call me your wife. We're not conventional people, anyway, we don't do the expected things." Meaning buying a home, raising children, having nine-to-five jobs. "We can *redefine* the labels."

"Honey," he said, sighing. "I'm here. I love you. Every day, I come home to you. I want to be with you. Isn't that enough?"

"I'm a writer. Words matter to me. I need to *name* things."

"What about the story? Doesn't our story matter to you? Do you want other people to write it based on what they think they know about us?"

I was bawling by this point. "Yes … I want … the story … and … I want the names!"

Don't you want to tell the world you love me?

Finally, a few months before my meeting with the surgeon, we compromised, buying a pair of matching silver commitment rings etched with vines that reached toward each other but did not touch.

There are few good men in true crime TV, except for investigators. There are no complex men, with as many flaws as strengths.

The killer husband is easy to hate. He is the stand-in for all of the troublesome men in women's lives: the abandoning fathers, the verbally abusive bosses, the boyfriends with explosive tempers, the unfaithful partners.

The killer husband is also easy to understand. A man's anger needs an outlet. My father's rage at finding himself responsible for supporting a large family found expression in constant grumbling about his boss, and in rare verbal and physical outbursts at his kids. Otherwise, he managed to submerge his frustrations in alcohol. My mother continually berated him for his financial recklessness, yet he hardly ever raised his voice in response.

I can see how a man might be tempted to solve his problems and vent his rage through murder. It makes sense. Violence belongs to men. A murderous man might push his wife off a cliff, make her strangulation look like the work of an intruder, stage her drowning in the bathtub as an accident or her overdose as a suicide. In all cases, he's had enough of her. Plus, he may want to marry his mistress, or nab a hefty life insurance payout that will settle his debts, or both. Some men kill their wives and children, forever freeing themselves from a burden they consider intolerable.

Andy would sooner cut off his own hand than raise it against me. He would do anything to preserve my life. But he knows what it's like to be pressured by a woman, to see the relationship differently than she does. Every time I confronted him about marriage, he resented me for it. He felt as if all of his love and devotion didn't mean as much to me as they should. I was essentially telling him his best wasn't good enough without the vows to back it up. That kind of hurt doesn't just go away. It's reawakened in times of crisis. It leads to anger.

There were no blow-out fights between Andy and me during my treatment for thyroid cancer. Even if we'd had the energy, it wouldn't have happened. Early in our relationship, I had insisted on a no-yelling rule. I'd grown up cringing at the sound of my mother's hollering. Displays of anger made my throat constrict, my heart quicken. I couldn't take it.

"But yelling is normal," Andy had argued.

"Yelling is destructive," I'd said. "It scares the hell out of me."

Andy finally acquiesced. Being human, he sometimes lost his temper and broke the rule. My tearful reactions left him feeling guilty—and angrier. We never discussed the option of simply stating, "I'm pissed at you." Andy probably thought that, too, would elicit my tears, and if he did think that, he was probably right.

When we started dating, I had assigned Andy the role of savior. It was his job to make up for my alcoholic parents, my miserable adolescence, the jerks I'd dated before him, and the toe-stubbings and petty insults that come with everyday life. Sometime during our first years together, when he observed, "Things land *so hard* on you," I didn't think, *He's right—and I'd better do something about it.* Instead, I sighed, awash in self-pity and the odd, dangerous contentment that comes with it. How right this man was about me, I marveled. How right he was *for* me. He was strong and I was vulnerable. The feminist within generously made room for my long-standing desire to be taken care of.

It didn't occur to me that if life's difficulties, large and small, landed *so hard* on me, my inability to cope would become burdensome to Andy. I didn't realize that the serious look on his face meant he was already feeling the weight, early on.

By the time my thyroid adventure got rolling, I had begun to understand that Andy was not my savior but a mortal, flawed human being. But I still had trouble picturing things from his point of view. I still viewed him as the strong one—my protector.

Since yelling wasn't allowed, his anger came out in less dramatic ways. Like exasperated sighs as we sat waiting for doctors and tests. "Why do they even bother making appointments if they can't keep them?" he muttered.

I was confused. Wasn't I the one who ought to be angry? I *was* angry when kept waiting, but then I was the patient. My understanding of Andy's experience in waiting rooms—trying to distract himself with copies of *People* and *Vermont Life* as he braced himself for my emergence, my announcement of the next appointment or test or procedure—would come much later.

Some appointments, he skipped. "You'll have to take the bus home," he'd say, more sharply than he might have intended. "I can't miss another half day of work. We can't afford it."

I was further confused when Andy's attitude about helping me through this time swung wildly from one end of the compassion spectrum to the other. "Why don't you *tell* me what you need? I can't guess," he'd say if he discovered me crying by myself, rattled by the latest piece of medical news or terrified of the next. "You make it so hard for me to support you." When I did seek his comfort, he often turned cold. "You need me too much. I can't do this."

In those moments, I shrank from him. I took to weeping in the shower with the water on full blast so he wouldn't hear me. Increasingly frightened, I needed his soft voice, needed him to literally hold my hand. To smooth out the finances. To take care of everything. And he did comfort me, holding me, stroking my hair, telling me how much he loved me, reassuring me that everything was going to be fine. But he showed his frustration, too, and I believed I couldn't bear to see it. I believed I needed him to carry everything with strength and kindness and endless patience. Until we knew I was OK, I needed him to need nothing for himself. Only my survival.

What neither of us could face was the fact that Andy was not only angry at doctors or fate or illness. He was angry at me, for becoming ill, for requiring even more care. He was angry that his fear of disease had been realized in the person he loved. He couldn't admit it to himself, much less to me. Had he been able to tell me, I don't think I would have believed him. I would have explained it away, turned it into some other story. It would be years before we could discuss it, longer still before I could forgive his anger and he could forgive my need.

Women viewers of true crime try to fathom the minds of men who murder. If a woman takes a life, we try to fathom her heart. The female killer is selfishly, outrageously acting on her own behalf, the way we expect men to act, the way we might want to. ID's *Deadly Women*, with all of its graphic recreations of poisonings and shootings and stabbings, sympathizes with the motives of female killers—money, sexual jealousy, rejection—but doesn't excuse their transgressions except in cases of severe mental illness. The show allows women viewers to indulge in violent fantasies, but by each story's end, it stresses the dire consequences of acting on those fantasies: nearly all of the women featured pay dearly for their crimes.

Deadly Women also speaks to the dangers of becoming wholly dependent on men, who often cannot or don't want to be the keepers of women's emotional health and physical survival. In our early days together, I would never have imagined that Andy would become resentful toward me. I doubt that when she married, my mother foresaw just how ill-suited my father was to the roles she hoped he would fulfill, the strong provider and tender partner she must have dreamed of as a girl. By the time of my thyroid surgeries, Andy's anger at me for needing more than he could give and my distress over his refusal to be my selfless protector didn't lead to violence, but they could have torn us apart.

As we counted down the days leading to my second surgery, we both became calmer, focusing on what lay ahead. I found Andy gazing at me with great love, saying things like, "I can't imagine my life without you," or "All I care about, the *only* thing, is seeing you get better. The rest is a fog." I knew he *was* imagining a life without me—what he would do, how he would go on. Even though I wasn't going to die: we kept reassuring each other of that.

I was glad he wasn't the one with cancer. I didn't want him to go through this—and I didn't want to be the partner left watching, waiting. I believed it was easier to be the patient than the caregiver; I still think so. I kept studying the commitment ring on my left hand, its shine, the little nicks and scratches it had accumulated in the past few months, the engraving of two vines almost, but not quite, becoming one.

The weekend before my second operation, Andy and I window-shopped in downtown Burlington. We spent a good hour in the art supply store. When writing proved frustrating, I turned to the wild freedom of acrylic abstracts. Since we couldn't paint the white walls in our rental, hanging my canvases allowed me to mark my territory in cobalt, smoky green, gold.

Andy wanted to buy all the colors of the world for me. "Would you like this?" he asked, picking up a wooden case with drawers containing oil paints, brushes, knives. "For Christmas?"

I saw the price: fifty dollars. Jesus. What was he thinking? Burton was over, and the holiday season was unlikely to yield new temp assignments. "Oh, you don't need to buy me anything like that. It's too expensive."

"Forget about that. Do you *like* it?"

I studied the solid blond wood. "It's very nice. Yes, I like it. I could try oils."

Everywhere, there were overpriced kits, slender tin boxes containing fancy drawing pencils, row after row of sketch pads and hardbound books of soft blank paper, drafting tables and easels, canvases of every size and shape stacked against the walls.

"Really, honey, whatever you picked out in here would be great. OK, maybe not soft pastels—they're hard to work with. Smudgy. But pretty much anything else."

Andy rolled his eyes. "I'm not going to remember that. I need a detailed list."

"All right! All right!"

We both feigned exasperation. He knew that art was one of my few sources of childlike glee. He would easily recall the items I pointed out to him, no list necessary, and on Christmas Eve I'd find one of them wrapped in blue snowflake paper. I knew that this year in particular, he wanted to give me exactly what I desired.

But I was tired suddenly. I no longer hungered for what was here.

"You ready to move on?" he asked.

"Yeah. Let's go."

Back home, Andy took me to bed, put his arms around me, and said, "Relax. I'll watch the world for you."

This. I wanted exactly this. Nothing more. Laying down my vigilance. Andy's body close to mine in the dimming November light. Weariness fuzzing through my veins, my eyes fluttering closed on the day. My awareness of what the world might bring softening all along its irregular edges, blurring, finally slipping into the black of black, the sleep that would turn to bright morning.

The second surgery went as smoothly as the first, three weeks earlier. I remember nothing from the hours before the procedure, except that I was starving: I'd been fasting since the previous night, and the surgeon was delayed by several hours on another case. They hooked me up to IV fluids so I wouldn't pass out.

When Dr. Sixtysomething finally appeared in pre-op, I turned to him with the beatific smile of the hunger-striking saint.

"Marcia, I can't tell you how sorry I am," he said, shaking his head at his own lateness.

"Ohhh, tha's all right," I drawled, too disoriented to be

disturbed by the presence of the man who would again go for my throat.

He was so goddamned sweet, this guy. There would be things I'd want him to be sorry for in the months to come. Showing up late for my surgery was never one of them. I understood emergencies.

Dr. Sixtysomething removed what was left of my thyroid. Three tiny tumors were found in the remaining lobe. As before, one night in the hospital for observation, and then I was released.

Remarkably, the scar stayed the same size. Still, doctors, nurses, and Andy were the only people I allowed to see it.

"Wow, it looks great. The surgeon did an amazing job," they kept saying. They were right; he *had* done an amazing job. Two surgeries, one slender scar? I should count myself lucky. I'd been dealt one of the most treatable forms of cancer. This was no brush with mortality, not really. I ought to be grateful, I told myself sternly. I had no right to complain.

I told no one that I grieved for the permanently lost, perfect surface of youth. That I hated how the scar announced my loss to every stranger on the street. How it carved a bright pink path across the intersection of voice, fear, blood, and breath. Dr. Sixtysomething was a caring, exceptionally skilled professional, but I couldn't help thinking again that the cut looked like the mark of an attacker. Not a maniac after all, but a methodical perpetrator.

Even as I reminded myself how lucky I was, I bought two more scarves: shiny, patterned in pinks and grays. I couldn't hide the fact of my cancer or the sight of my injury from myself, but I could hide them from everyone else.

Chapter 7

The Danger Next Door

Randy owned a farm not far from my childhood home. He and my father drank together at Randy's big farmhouse, in winter fishing shanties, at our kitchen table, and in our basement family room.

Mom didn't like Randy—his loud voice, the dirt he tracked onto her clean floors, or the way he and my father sometimes drank more together than they might have apart. "Those two, just egging each other on," she would grumble.

My mother did like Randy's wife, Shirley. Sometimes the four of them gathered at the farmhouse and drank late into the night. Once, my parents brought me with them, and forgot to take me when they headed home. I had fallen asleep in the den.

Randy was big. Big hands, floppy unkempt hair that got in his eyes, big voice, big laugh. A shambling giant to a small child. Once, when I was five years old, my mother, my sisters, and I were walking from the lake up the dirt road toward our house. My sisters and I wore one-piece swimsuits. Mom wore shorts and a tank top. She didn't swim; I don't think she knew how. "There's Randy," Mom said, disdain in her voice.

He was getting out of his pickup in our driveway. I took my towel from my shoulders and wrapped it around my torso. I don't remember if my sisters did the same.

I didn't know how I could be sex. I didn't know what sex was. My sisters told me not to put stuffed animals I designated as boys in the same bunk bed with Raggedy Ann, but they never said why. I knew to keep Barbie's clothes on before putting her away in the closet. Nobody had to tell me that she would be ashamed if left naked, even in the dark. Nobody had to tell me to cover myself all the way from my neck to the tops of my thighs around Randy. And still, the towel didn't feel like it was enough.

After Randy got a divorce, he began coming to our house by himself. He became fixated on one of my sisters. She was about sixteen; Randy was in his forties. He asked my father if he could date her. I wonder how drunk Randy was when he asked this, or if he was perfectly sober and thought this was a reasonable request.

The way my mother told it to my sisters, probably thinking I wasn't listening or couldn't understand, I knew from her contemptuous tone that Randy had crossed some shameful line. My father told Randy no. For once, he had done something right in Mom's eyes. He was almost a hero.

Mom was right, I didn't understand. I didn't know that Randy should have been kept out of our house after that.

My mother scoffed at how Randy knelt on our kitchen floor once, picking up my sister's leather clog and holding it. "He was cradling it in his hands!" she said, snorting. Like she couldn't believe it. Like he was just a fool. But not even a woman with anger like hers could ever raise her voice to him. That would be rude.

She complained about how Randy parked his truck on the road in front of our house one night, with a drinking buddy who wasn't my father on the passenger side. Maybe a drunk cousin; he had a number of those. "With the headlights shining right through the living-room window!" She said it like it was an amazing fact, a curiosity. Like my sisters should be disgusted. Not like any of them, even the object of Randy's desire, should be afraid. Not like my father should have done something about it. Not like Mom should have told Randy he wasn't welcome in our house, since my father never would.

It is still with shame that I watch *Forensic Files*, looking for unobscured images of the dead. I pause before I turn the channel to this show, taking a moment to acknowledge I have not shaken my need to see the very worst things that can happen to women.

On one episode, a woman is stabbed in her bed over one hundred times. We see only part of the crime scene—one leg, streaked with blood, plus smears of blood on walls. We are told the victim has been posed by the killer with her legs spread to suggest a sexual assault, yet the autopsy reveals she was not raped. Police eventually zero in on a young man who lived in the same apartment complex at the time of the murder. His window gave him a direct line of sight into the victim's home. He became obsessed, masturbating as he watched her.

Police determine that the man crawled in through her kitchen window while she was out and waited for her to come home, possibly hiding in her bedroom closet. They believe he intended to rape her, but she fought him off with more force than he had expected. About half of the stab wounds were inflicted postmortem, indicating the depths of his obsession.

What I find most disturbing about male offenders is their ability to fixate on a particular woman. The man on that episode of *Forensic Files* probably chose his victim simply because she was there, right in front of him. Maybe hers was the only apartment he could look into from the safety of his own. But I find it hard to understand how he began with window peeping and went on to develop a full-blown sexual obsession. She was a stranger, but the relationship between them must have been very real in his mind. Did he think of her as a potential girlfriend? Or did he always think of her as his victim?

He is like the stalker who targets the female news anchor or the former high school classmate—a woman with whom he has had little or no contact. He is like the serial rapist who singles out each victim because she resembles someone important from his past, or because something about her sparks a sexual fantasy, or because he knows when she will be alone without anyone to protect her. The seemingly random details of a woman's appearance and lifestyle give such men purpose.

More than anything, though, it is her proximity that appeals to him. She becomes his target simply by appearing in his field of vision.

I don't know exactly when I first saw the original 1975 *Jaws* movie poster: an illustration of a naked woman swimming, about to be devoured by the much-larger-than-life great white, with teeth like knives. As a child, whatever my age, I wouldn't have known that the real animal's teeth are triangular, not flat and elongated like kitchen blades. I would have believed the image, every aspect of it.

When I look at the poster now, I find myself instinctively hunching over at the sight of that woman, her breast pointing at the beast that is many times her size. The illustration feels very familiar.

I remember that the 1983 summer release of *Jaws 3-D* brought with it a media blitz. I never saw any of the *Jaws* movies as a kid; I didn't have to. The TV trailers were enough to make me scared to swim in the lake, though at twelve, I knew perfectly well that sharks didn't live in fresh water. The illustration for the 3-D movie poster features male and female water-skiers about to succumb to the shark. Of course, a woman is its first victim, her body already submerged, dwarfed by the approaching fin. In case we might forget it, there is a second, gigantic rendering of the shark—that mouth full of knives from the original, looming over all.

As my siblings began leaving home, Randy's obsession never shifted to another of my father's daughters, not that I know of. It seemed he had learned to look without saying anything he shouldn't, to take in the sight of teenage beauties without fondling anyone's footwear.

But as the size of the family continued to dwindle, Randy noticed me, the summer I was twelve.

I was getting a glass of iced tea from the fridge, quiet so as not to interrupt Mom's conversation with Randy. They were drinking beer at the kitchen table, probably waiting for my father to come home from work. I moved almost noiselessly, head bowed, lips set in a small smile so that Mom couldn't accuse me later of looking glum in front of company. "What's *your* problem?" she sneered whenever one of her daughters made a face or just appeared unhappy. I never had an answer for her. On this afternoon, I was wearing shorts and the torturous training bra under my T-shirt. The device that, in trying to contain the body, made it obvious.

"Your little girl's growing up," Randy said. I kept my back to him. I felt his eyes there.

"Yeah," Mom said. "She's really filling out."

Why was it summer? I longed for thick corduroy pants and a heavy, cable-knit sweater to obscure the bra's tight-packed bumps, the telltale outline of its straps hooked across my back. I wondered if Randy could see the outline. I wondered why Mom invited him to look. Why she didn't simply say, "I know, she'll be in seventh grade this year," and leave my body out of it. Why she pointed out to Randy that the development he had found so enticing in her older daughter was beginning to happen to her youngest. My skin was fine pastry. I was a confection, waiting for some man to take the first bite.

"Do you know what happens to young girls?" Mom asked me when I was in my mid-teens. "Do you know what men do?"

When she told me stories of murder and rape from her true crime books, my mother forgot she was my mother in those moments, forgot that I was her highly sensitive, anxious daughter.

The stories about sexual assault disturbed me most. I begged her to spare me the details, but nothing I said could stop her from telling me about the man who bit a woman all over her body before killing her, or about the gang rape of a thirteen-year-old girl.

I grew up terrified of rape. Consciously, I feared the scenarios from Mom's stories: the stranger creeping into my bedroom at night or abducting me from a darkened street. Even in our tiny town, it seemed possible.

When I was fifteen, I made the mistake of watching a two-part TV movie about Ted Bundy, *The Deliberate Stranger*, with Mom—my attempt to bond over the kind of story that preoccupied her, and to satisfy my curiosity about the notorious killer who made the evening news with appeal after appeal, evading the electric chair.

The Deliberate Stranger was just a movie, I told myself. My sisters would have been eager to watch it with Mom. I don't remember discussing the movie with my mother. Drinking beer, she would have become less coherent as the program ran. When the credits rolled after the conclusion of Part Two, I suppose we both murmured something about how "terrible" it all was, and went to bed. After five or six beers and Ativan, the medication she took to sleep, Mom probably sank into a heavy slumber. I probably lay awake. I don't recall.

But decades after that single viewing, I remembered Mark

Harmon as Bundy, carrying a woman's corpse through the snow, her hand dangling as he walks. I remembered Harmon as Bundy bludgeoning a young woman in her bed, blood splattering the walls of her room in a sorority house. I remembered nightmares in the weeks after watching the movie: Harmon/Bundy at my bedroom window, smiling as he calmly set about prying it open.

From adolescence onward, I thought that rape was not something I would want to survive. I could not imagine how any woman might endure the trauma, how she might live with the terror that it would happen again. If the rapist didn't kill me, I figured I would kill myself. In either case, I would not live in a body violated by a man.

My father did not even need to touch me to harm me, or to make me want to harm myself.

Below consciousness was the fear that my father would enter my bedroom one night. My nightmares of Bundy transferred the unthinkable to the irrational: I couldn't lock my bedroom door if I couldn't admit why I needed to. But Bundy was under heavy guard on death row in Florida. It was safer to fear him.

Late at night, near the end of my senior year of high school, I plotted my escape.

I sat in my narrow little-girl twin bed, knees drawn up under the covers. A desk lamp on the bookcase sheathed me in a circle of crisp, hot light. My parents had already gone to their rooms; Mom, submerged under the combined effects of her sleeping pill and that evening's alcohol intake, would never know I was still up. And if she did know, what did I care?

I was eighteen. I had the golden ticket in hand, a full-tuition academic scholarship to the University of Vermont. I was going to major in psychology; I would learn to save people from themselves.

My grades hadn't been perfect, but they were close enough. I'd stayed holed up in this room, writing papers and application essays, studying Latin verbs and SAT vocabulary flash cards. It had taken tremendous effort to open the door to my future. UVM was in Burlington, just forty-five minutes from Swanton, but a world away.

In my last years of high school, as the pressure to achieve mounted, Mom began to let me go. When I made feeble attempts to clear the table after dinner, I knew she would stop me. "I'll get these," she'd say. "You go and study."

It was all she had left to give me: the chance to steal my own life.

Mom never taught me the basics of housekeeping. She knew I wasn't interested. She didn't approve of my ambivalence toward motherhood. "Everybody wants kids, Marcia. Even movie stars."

Yet she was helping me to leave her. To become less and less like her. To pursue professional success instead of dreaming of starting a family of my own. For a brief time, she faced who I was.

All I had left to give her was to stay with her in this house—a sacrifice unthinkable to both of us. I had to shut out the image of her alone with my father, without even the distant presence of her last daughter, bedroom door firmly closed at the far end of the house.

I munched one Oreo after another, poring over the UVM catalogue. I loved the sharp orderliness of the course descriptions: dry, no-nonsense, laid out in precise columns. I wanted to inhale that cool intellectual rigor, breathe it into my blood. I wanted to be all high-flown thought, no more messy emotion. I was going to leave this house, and college would release and refine the dynamic, charming, brilliant person who had been locked within me all these years, the person my parents could not have raised. I did not yet know the term *in loco parentis*, but it describes exactly what I desired: I wanted college to parent me.

What a release, what a thrill—to leave this room forever. Deliverance. Living, not dying.

College did give me the intellectual foundation I had hoped for. I learned to analyze information, to defend my ideas, to look for dark truths in history and in people. But college didn't change me: I was still a shy, scared girl who had to work up the courage to speak in class.

I spent the first two years in dorms, where locked, formidable outer doors and the presence of many residents above and below my floor made me feel safe from intruders. The apartment I shared with two women friends my junior and senior years was on the first floor, and I didn't trust our door's dead bolt or the locks on the windows. I was nervous when walking home alone after late nights at the library, but I was specifically terrified of being raped in my own bed.

When both roommates spent nights away, staying with boyfriends or at home during school vacations, I panicked. My bedroom window faced a dark alley, secluded by hedges. It cranked out—relatively easy to pry open, it seemed to me—and I could think of no way to secure it other than shutting the flimsy lock. I focused on securing the door instead. I looped my bike lock around the doorknob, fastening the other end to a knob on my bureau. I once tried pushing the bureau to block the door, but found I couldn't budge it. It didn't occur to me that if someone entered through the window after I'd barricaded myself in the room, I would be trapped. I bought Mace to protect myself both at home and on the street, but got rid of it once I realized it was more likely to be torn from my hand and used against me than to enable me to fend off an attacker.

Alone in the apartment, I lay awake most of the night, unable to turn out the light, convinced the rustling of leaves was the sound of someone quietly removing the screen from my window. I watched the crack under the door for shifting shadows that could indicate the approach of a man in a black ski mask.

My roommates had both been molested as children, yet they were mystified by my fear. "There's being careful, and then there's being paranoid," one tried to explain. I didn't know why they weren't as terrified as I was, or even more so. Weren't they afraid that what had happened when they were little girls could happen again? It would take me years to understand: For them, the tension had broken. I was still bracing for an attack.

Chapter 8

All the Rage

A fter the second thyroid surgery, I was a haunted house. Empty of everything except the memory of who I was before. The spirit of my former self rattled and cried, enraged, aggrieved. It wanted to reinhabit this body. It didn't understand why it couldn't. The person I was now lived here uneasily. This house was not quite mine, not with the ghost tapping on the doors. Medicine asserted its unquestioned authority, took over the property for a time, and then abandoned it.

Medicine could come by again any time it wanted. It knew the way.

It was as if I needed a third surgery, a reconstruction. I needed the surgeon to rebuild what he tore out. Not to replace the thyroid; I was told I could live without that. What else did he take, exactly? Whatever was lost besides flesh when the throat was cut. Whatever was wept out silently in the blood.

I tried to imagine myself on the operating table, the surgeon and his team standing over me, but it didn't seem real. I couldn't see the cutting, the blood. There was no conscious memory of anything except absence: perfect blackness, perfect stillness, perfect silence. It seemed that I died for an hour, and then came back. Twice.

The year before my surgeries, Andy and I went to see *Capote*, about the author's investigation of the 1959 murders of an entire family in Kansas, and the book he wrote about the crime, *In Cold Blood*, often referred to as the genesis of the true crime genre. I loved movies about writers. I didn't know the film would depict the killings. I quickly turned away from the scene in which Perry Smith watches blood gush from Herb Clutter's slashed throat.

The next image from the film was the one that haunted me: Smith hobbling up the staircase with his shotgun to kill the mother, Bonnie, and teenage daughter, Nancy, both tied up in their beds. His limp made his ascent slower, creepier. For weeks afterward, when I headed from my darkened living room to our bedroom, I crept sideways up the stairs, looking back to make sure Smith's ghost wasn't following me with his gun.

Despite my nighttime fears, I was curious about the book. Words were easier to take than films. Still, I had to read it during several visits to Barnes and Noble, slipping a copy off the shelf and settling into an armchair to find the point where I'd left off. I didn't want it in my house.

After my surgeries, we rented the DVD of *Capote*. I told Andy it would be all right, the film wouldn't bother me the way it did the first time. I didn't tell him it was the cut throat of Herb Clutter I wanted to see. He was surprised when I kept my eyes on the TV screen during the scene. "I needed to see it," I explained afterward. Andy nodded. He knew I was referring to my surgeries, though he was still mystified. The film doesn't show the drawing of the blade, only the immediate aftermath: the man writhing, wide-eyed, gasping for breath, blood spurting from the wound. Of course, it was nothing like the precise control of the OR. But I needed this image. I had no other.

I came upstairs to bed that night without looking back.

I picked fights with Andy: Why wouldn't he marry me? As if I didn't know that my drama was too much for him, I was too much for him. I pushed him until he admitted that he was overwhelmed. He was as stuck in anger as I was. He countered: How could I possibly be worrying about weddings? What were we going to do about money for our everyday, ever-growing expenses, now that I was unemployed? Later, I cried in the shower so he wouldn't hear me. I came to bed angry. I woke up angry.

I told Vanessa, my therapist, how furious I was. A kind, slight, soft-spoken woman, she was not the sort to suggest pillow pounding. She made connections. She validated. "The cancer experience infantilized you," she observed.

Yes, I agreed, it turned me into a big fucking baby.

"What do I do now?" I asked.

She must have given me practical suggestions; she always did. Probably speaking up for myself, asking for what I needed. The ABCs of empowerment. I left her office and was instantly embroiled again in rage, my head swarming with thoughts of endless appointments and inconclusive tests and mysterious procedures, and any advice she might have given me was swept clean from my memory.

My psychiatrist could keep me supplied with antidepressants, try different drugs to combat the intractable insomnia I'd had since childhood, and it all helped to some degree. Depression, anxiety, and insomnia were treatable conditions. Rage and fear were not.

I was furious at my body's betrayal. But I had a till-death-do-we-part situation here. Should I scream at my reflection in the mirror? I was much too terrified. Instead, I begged my body: *Let me live and I won't say a word against you. I will swallow all the meds they tell me to swallow and get all the tests they tell me to*

*get and consent to whatever they deem necessary. I will do anything
if you let me live.*

I was alone with this weird kind of cancer that no one
seemed to take seriously now that it had been cut out of me.
Alone with the breathlessness of slipping past death—the cold,
sick feeling at the back of the neck. Unable to explain the mess
inside my head, the dread that ran through my veins. My body
and mind were completely spent from bracing for the next sharp
edge. A weariness that felt permanent, though I knew it couldn't
be. Bed to couch, then back to bed.

I wrote long rants in my journal, then scribbled over them
and slashed the pages with the point of my pen. I threw hardcover books across the living room, tossed forks and knives clattering into the sink, slammed the bathroom door. I pounded my
thighs with both fists. Nothing touched that dark cavity inside
me that only understood violence.

But I wasn't a victim. No one hurt me. Jesus, no one took
anything from me except cancer. And my thyroid, but who cared
about that? I was not really this angry. If I *was* this angry, I must
be crazy. If I was crazy, no one else was to blame except me.
Maybe I was to blame for the cancer, too. Look how horribly
negative I was. Did bad thoughts turn cells black? Was I trying
to kill myself every day with my sarcasm, with my tendency to
dismiss everything and everyone as stupid?

The first of my mother's hospitalizations I remember took place
when I was nine. It had to do with "female trouble." That was
the only explanation she ever gave me. Once home, she showed
me her hysterectomy incision, the red edges of her flesh cruelly
bound by black thread. I shuddered.

"This is how you were born," she reminded me, adding that
my brother and sister also came into the world by caesarean. The
hysterectomy was the fourth cut in the same place.

I saw that being a woman meant wound on wound, injury

upon injury. It meant being stilled as my mother had been stilled on the operating table, as she lay pinned by pain on the living-room couch. She wasn't angry anymore. The surgeon had taken even that from her. Until she recovered, and had the strength again to raise her voice.

Now I had to take permission to be angry. Women are told every day of their lives that it is wrong for them to be angry. Even when they are wounded more than once in the same place. Look how things turned out for my mother. Fury ate her guts.

Being angry and saying nothing felt like dying. Being angry and screaming about it would have made me my mother. Being angry and doing nothing about it except screaming killed my mother, inflaming her insides until her body gave out. Fury was a growth devouring me cell by cell. I would have grabbed a kitchen knife and excised it with my own hands if I could.

Too late. It was in my throat. Blood, lungs, hair, brain. The blackened walls of my atria and ventricles. The exploded red star of my solar plexus. At night, tears and small, stifled screams, writing it down all-caps furious.

Nothing could kill this motherfucker. Not until the day something finally killed me.

The fury was a ball lodged in my windpipe, exactly where my scar lay. I couldn't speak because of the fury. The bright pink scar spoke for me. It said, *All better now. I am small and neat, proof of the surgeon's skill and efficiency.*

Even Andy looked at the fresh incision and marveled, "It hardly looks like anything happened." I thought it looked like I'd been attacked.

They told me the scar would fade over time. I wanted it to fade so that no one could ever spot it and say, "Oh, my God. What happened to you?" I did not want anyone feeling sorry for me. Of course, no one had ever commented on it. But what if someone did? What would I say? That my sweet jolly-grandpa surgeon left the mark of a predator? It wouldn't make any sense.

He was not a predator or a thief. But still, I imagined a thief running his knife along the edge of a window screen and slipping in through the incision. I meant *slit*. No, I meant *hole*. He would take what he could in the dark and leave the way he entered.

Next morning, a woman would wake and find the cut screen. She would wheel around. Nothing would appear to be missing. How could she call the police? How could she explain that she felt something invisible was gone? She couldn't describe what had been taken. She couldn't even give it a name.

I didn't want the scar to fade. I wanted it to say what I could not. I wanted it to grow pinker until it was full saturated scarlet. Until it bled again. Blood frightened everyone. That was its purpose. The precision of the cut was irrelevant.

I didn't see Dr. Sixtysomething again after the second surgery. Another doctor took out my sutures. Minus a thyroid, I was considered endocrinology's problem from then on. They sent me to radiology for the final and simplest step in my cancer treatment, the single dose of radioactive iodine in the form of a large capsule I swallowed easily. No sharps involved.

I was left with the strange sense that the surgeon and I shared something extraordinarily intimate. I wasn't finished with him.

"Don't *worry!*" he had told me repeatedly. His seriousness on the day he delivered my diagnosis was an aberration. Otherwise, he was his merry, chuckling self. I thought of our first meeting, when I was deeply frightened and let it show on my face, as if I were a child again, being ever-so-gently scolded for my worry-wart tendencies.

How to complain about a doctor—and not just any doctor, but a *surgeon*—who radiated warmth? I couldn't. I didn't. What I wouldn't put words to for years was that warmth was not necessarily empathy. Discouraging the expression of feelings was certainly not empathy. For weeks after the second surgery, I kept calling otolaryngology, trying my damnedest to make myself their problem again. I knew I wouldn't get through to Dr. Sixtysomething; I wouldn't have known what to say if, by some miracle, they put him on the phone. Instead I was trying to get something from his staff. I wasn't sure what I was angling for. Maybe answers to questions I was unable to voice, questions they couldn't answer even if I could voice them. Maybe compassion.

If I couldn't get answers or compassion, I'd settle for drugs. Drugs to quiet this anger for at least a few hours a day.

"I need Vicodin; I'm having headaches," I told a nurse. I didn't tell her that Excedrin worked just fine.

"Did you know Vicodin can *cause* headaches?" she asked, voice bright with kindergarten-teacher condescension.

I called back: Were there reports from the surgeries, descriptions of the procedures? I asked another nurse. Yes, she said. Why hadn't someone sent me the reports? I demanded. Why did I have to ask? The nurse didn't explain, just assured me they'd be mailed to me. It occurred to me later that they probably didn't hand them out to most patients—that most patients didn't want to read them. Well, I bloody well wanted to read them. I didn't want the real story hidden from me.

I ripped open the envelope so fast it almost tore in half. Sinking into the worn, beige living-room sofa, I began to read. I forgot I was surrounded by my shelves of books with their red and green and orange spines, my framed photos of Andy and me from our trip to San Francisco two years earlier (those unreal, bright-blue, optimistic skies), my big, splotchy, cobalt-gold-and-white acrylic painting that looked like Pollock got drunk, ate Monet, and threw him up on the canvas. I wasn't here. I was back in the OR, floating above what couldn't possibly be my body, witnessing a strange rite that looked more like sacrifice than saving:

PROCEDURE REPORT
SERVICE DATE: 11/06/2006

NARRATIVE: The patient was identified and consent was obtained. The patient was brought to the operating room. Anesthesia was induced. After an adequate level of a general anesthetic was obtained, the patient was orally intubated and placed supine on the operating table … The neck was prepped and draped in the usual sterile fashion. A low midline neck incision of approximately 9 cm was used. It was marked out in a preexisting skin crease and injected with 1% lidocaine with 1:100,000 epinephrine. After an adequate time for vasoconstriction, a #10 blade was used to incise through the skin and subcutaneous tissues down to the platysma muscle. Subplatysmal flaps were raised superiorly and inferiorly. The median raphe of the strap muscles was identified and separated in the midline. Minimal bleeding was controlled with bipolar cautery. The larger vessels were clamped and ligated with 3-0 silk ties. The right thyroid lobe was then skeletonized, dissecting carefully around, first, the inferior border. A small parathyroid was found inferiorly, slightly adherent to the thyroid capsule. This was carefully dissected free, preserving its blood supply. The superior lobe of the thyroid was then dissected. It was very elongated, riding high in the neck, but was completely dissected free and separated from the surrounding tissues. The superior pole vessel was clamped and ligated. The nodule was easily palpated in the mid inferior portion of the gland. Following it around posteriorly, the recurrent laryngeal nerve was identified and followed deep to the specimen. The specimen was carefully delivered, preserving the nerve in the depths of the field. The tracheal attachments were divided and the thyroid isthmus then divided using the pencil cautery. The specimen was marked with a marking stitch in the mid anterior isthmus and sent to pathology for frozen section. The frozen sections came back consistent with a follicular lesion. Therefore, the surgery was terminated at this point. A Hemovac drain was placed. The platysma muscle was then reapproximated using interrupted 4-0 Monocryl sutures and a running subcuticular 4-0 Prolene suture was used for skin closure. Telfa and Tegaderm were placed as a dressing. The patient was extubated and brought to the PACU in good condition. Dr. [Sixtysomething] was present and participated in the entire case.

ESTIMATED BLOOD LOSS: Minimal.

I finished reading and realized my hand was covering my mouth.

I thought I knew how that poor stinking frog in high school biology class felt. I was as cold as a dead, wet amphibian. This was a masterwork of the passive voice. Dr. Sixtysomething and the doctor assisting him and the whole Disney crew of cheery OR personnel: it sounded like nobody laid a finger on me, yet somehow the surgery got done.

Years later, a woman doctor gently explained to me that they would have taken off my gown after I was anesthetized, leaving me naked under the surgical drapes. Reading the report, I had no idea I'd been undressed while unconscious. I'd gone under wearing the gown and woke up in what I'd assumed to be the same gown.

The report on the second surgery went much the same way as the first—except it mentioned two lymph nodes being removed, one containing a tumor.

I got back on the phone. I must have sounded especially persuasive or extra upset, or maybe litigious. The miracle occurred: they put the surgeon himself on the line. Like babbling prayers out loud and suddenly finding yourself patched through to God. It rattled me. "You—you didn't tell me about the lymph nodes!" I spluttered.

"I did tell you, Marcia," Dr. Sixtysomething replied softly.

When? When I was in the hospital bed, whacked out on pain-killers? How could I not remember, whacked out or not? How will I ever know if you are correct?

And yet why, why *am I so furious at you? You saved my life. You certainly never meant me any harm.*

I couldn't say any of this.

Why, after hanging up, did I slam my fist against the wall? Why did I moan with sobs as I did it?

Why this ball lodged in my windpipe?

Grateful. I should have been grateful.

The anesthesiologist, also a man, knocked me out cold. I never saw the surgeon coming.

Grateful. I should have been grateful.

Chapter 9

Invasion

S ixteen months after my thyroid surgeries, my life with Andy had settled into the unfamiliar state of nothing-wrongness.

Our relationship survived my cancer diagnosis and its aftermath. We didn't talk about it much, out of some combination of superstition (mine), sadness about what I'd endured (his), and shame over the anger my illness produced (both of us). I'd stopped pushing for marriage, not because I'd changed my mind, but because I didn't want to create more discord after what we'd just been through. We both wanted to enjoy this time after our shared ordeal, so this period of peace was in part something we consciously created.

But it was also fate smiling on us. Finally, our finances were running smoothly. We were both temping, Andy was teaching guitar and banjo students at our home, and I was steadily building my list of editing clients. I'd been called back to Burton and stayed until the work ran out again. The temp agency then reassigned me to another hooray-for-youth company, a hip sports-oriented marketing firm. The employees were as kind and patient as the guys at Burton, and bless them, many were in their thirties, like me.

I left my scarf collection where it had been for months, in the closet. The thyroidectomy scar had faded dramatically, to a shade of pink only a little darker than my natural skin tone. I still didn't like seeing it in the mirror every day, but leaving it open to view had become a point of pride. It was a medical record as surely as any piece of paper. Proof of a life saved, a life worth saving.

In true crime TV, the woman who is getting everything she wants out of life is headed for a downfall. I've heard essentially the same narration, over and over: *Susie appeared to have it all: a loving husband, two beautiful children, a thriving career. No one knew her marriage was in trouble.* This is our cue that Susie's husband is about to kill her, or she's about to kill him, or Susie's secret lover is about to kill the husband, or the husband's secret lover is about to kill Susie. In each of these scenarios, the family is shattered, the children suffer, and Susie is either a perpetrator or a passive victim who doesn't heed warning signs.

I'm sure I'm not the only female viewer who takes black-hearted pleasure in watching women's perfect lives fall apart. The state of nothing-wrongness never lasts. From the bliss of the wedding day, it's all downhill. The narrators of these stories, whether male or female, often strike an unmistakably satisfied tone: *Her façade was about to crumble.* I can't be the only one who's looking for flaws in women's marriages and in their mothering, two endeavors I never took on myself.

Women often judge each other mercilessly for their lifestyle choices. If you can't get your boyfriend to marry you, you are pitiable, and if you're childless by choice, you are selfish. I've gotten these messages in subtle and not-so-subtle form: Sometimes people look confused when I introduce Andy as my partner and not as my husband. My mother freely admitted she had too many kids, but thought something was wrong with me if I didn't want children at all. So it's a kind of payback when I roll my eyes at true crime stories in which women marry men who are obviously wrong for them, or have more children than they can handle. *You think you're going to change him?* I sneer silently. *Have you ever heard of birth control?* Part of the wicked fun of watching true crime is that women's lives are laid bare, allowing female viewers to pick apart the intimate details, and to predict the trouble that's coming.

I like evaluating the choices made by women in true crime stories. But sometimes I can relate to them too well. These women are like heat-seeking missiles, searching out men who might be husband material. I can't claim I didn't do the same thing with Andy.

In true crime, women refer unironically to fairy tales: Prince Charming, weddings fit for a princess, happily-ever-after unions. Successful professional women are no less susceptible to the Disney notion of romance. It doesn't seem to occur to any of these women that bad things can happen even with Prince Charming standing by your side.

After my cancer diagnosis, I knew better. Ring or no ring, I had my prince, and I got bad news anyway. But I still thought marriage would mean that Andy was finally ready to be my end-lessly self-sacrificing partner. I had no idea that his devotion was about to be put to the test once more.

During this period of nothing-wrongness, out of nowhere, my left calf grew an enormous lump, like a baseball in hardness and dimension.

I made an appointment with Clarissa, the nurse practitioner who'd found my thyroid nodule. Surely it was nothing serious. It was just *weird*. Clarissa would get me to laugh about it. Me and my amusing medical oddities.

She came in, plump and smiling as always, her curly blonde hair bobbing as she approached the exam table, where I sat with my pant leg rolled up. She took one look at the baseball and said, "I can't say for sure, but it looks like a blood clot."

Fuck. Clarissa's always right.

"I'm calling the vascular lab at the hospital. They'll do an ultrasound. You should go today," Clarissa said in her even-keeled manner. That was one of the great things about her. I could have cancer, or I could have mild dermatitis, and in either case she'd speak to me in her assured, reasonable tone of voice. No brisk, put-on cheerfulness, no minimizing or dramatizing.

"What do they do for a blood clot?" I asked, steeling myself.

I could see her weighing how much to tell me. "Anticoagulants ... But wait, OK? Wait and see what they say."

I hobbled into the waiting room, where Andy sat engrossed in *Glamour*. What on earth had he found in there?

"Honey ..." I began softly. Andy knows what "honey" with nothing after it means. He dropped the magazine.

"It's probably nothing," I lied, "but Clarissa says it might be a blood clot."

"Blood clot?"

"I'm sure it's fine, but we have to go to the hospital. For an ultrasound."

"Now?"

"Now."

At the vascular lab, a very young sonographer *(God, what is she, twenty? Is that possible?)* matter-of-factly informed us that I did indeed have a blood clot, a deep vein thrombosis (DVT) running from mid-calf to mid-thigh.

There was no time to process this information. I was sent to the ER, where a nurse, a vivacious young woman who seemed barely older than the sonographer, taught me to give myself injections of Lovenox, an anticoagulant, by pinching my belly fat and pushing the needle straight in.

"That didn't hurt at all," I said, amazed.

The nurse grinned. "Nah, nothing to it."

Andy and I went home late that night, rattled but reassured that the problem had been quickly diagnosed and treatment had already begun. We were like the innocent couples of true crime programs, who all too readily believe their troubles are over once the restraining order for the crazy ex is in place, or the gun-toting neighbor is locked up. The ex will disregard the piece of paper and show up on the couple's doorstep with a baseball bat. The neighbor will get out of jail early and fetch a rifle from his garage before he heads next door for a little talk about property lines. Andy and I should have learned from my cancer that diseases are like criminals who aren't satisfied with doing just a little damage. They are out to ruin your life.

A few days later, Andy brought me to the hospital for my follow-up appointment with Elise, a nurse practitioner in hematology.

Elise was inordinately cheerful. A petite, middle-aged woman with cropped black hair, she was naturally upbeat; her smile was unselfconscious, not put on along with her white coat. I immediately felt at ease with her. She ordered a computed tomography (CT) scan of my chest. They wanted a look at my lungs, she explained, because clots in the leg could travel. I just nodded as I always did in the presence of medical personnel. To myself, I thought: *I have no chest pain, none at all, so how could I have clots in my lungs?*

Andy stayed for most of the appointment, then left for work. I had a great excuse for missing shifts at my temp job, but one of us had to keep the income rolling. He threw me a worried/ guilty look. "I'll pick you up at, what do you think, four?" We had to figure out the timing now. We were the last two people in America without cell phones.

I waved him away. "Yeah, four. Go on, *please*, I'm fine."

Clad in a gown, I lay down on the long, narrow bench that slides you through the *O* of the scanner and held still for half an hour while the machine took X-ray images from various angles. Afterward, the friendly tech looked serious when I asked about the results. "A doctor has to review them first," she said. "I'm sorry I can't tell you more."

"That's all right," I said, although I was starting to get nervous.

I put my clothes back on and waited alone in a tiny room between the dressing area and a door marked CLINICIANS ONLY BEYOND THIS POINT. An enormous flat-screen TV blared overhead: Judge Judy shouting at hapless defendants over unpaid rent, property damage, broken promises. Everyone looked guilty. Everyone looked terrified. Several women cried.

I looked in vain for a remote, for power or volume-control buttons on the TV. I didn't dare leave. The longer I waited, the more likely it seemed that something was wrong.

The courtroom screeching continued. Twenty minutes passed. Forty.

I was thinking about smashing the plasma screen with the heel of my shoe when Elise appeared, beckoning me into the clinicians-only area. We stood in a hallway.

"Marcia," Elise began quietly. "You have bilateral pulmonary emboli. That means clots in both lungs. We need to admit you."

I didn't panic. I didn't protest. "For how long?"

She paused. "It varies. Probably four to five days."

"Four to five days." A heaviness spread through my belly, anchoring me to the square of linoleum on which I stood, facing Elise. I met her gaze unwaveringly. I felt the hospital closing in; I understood that I was being trapped so I wouldn't die.

I was more worried about Andy than myself. How would he take this? He was picking me up in—I looked at my watch—ten minutes, at four o'clock.

"Andy's pulling the car around front," I told Elise. "I have to meet him."

She blinked at me. "But you can't go out there. We have to get you a room. There's ... well, there's a procedure to all of this, and I—"

"I *have* to meet him. He doesn't know any of this. We don't have cell phones."

"OK," Elise said. "We'll go together, then." We took the elevator down to the ground-floor level, and she hung back while I went outside.

I spotted the Subaru at the curb. For a moment, I thought of just getting in, telling Andy, "Everything checked out, let's go home."

I opened the passenger-side door and leaned down. He looked at me. "What are you doing? You're not getting in?" His face darkened. "You're not getting in."

"I'm going to be all right, but they have to admit me. I have blood clots in my lungs."

He just stared at me, openmouthed.

"I'm going to be all right. Elise is with me. I'll make her wait until you park the car. We'll be at registration."

I could see him struggling to contain his anger. Not anger at me, I knew. Anger at my illness. My *latest* illness ... *Depression and cancer weren't enough? She has to get something else?* I could practically see his thoughts.

He put his head in his hands.

I would have done anything, anything in the world short of lying, to have spared him that moment.

"I'll meet you there," he choked out, shutting the door and pulling away from the curb.

On the ward, my bed was at the far end of the room, away from the door. If I leaned over far enough, I could glimpse the softening April sky through a narrow window.

An ancient woman lay in the next bed, beyond a white nylon curtain hanging from metal rings. She was either heavily asleep or semiconscious. She would stay that way the entire time I was there. I never knew what condition she suffered from.

I felt trapped in this tiny half of a tiny room. With a bureau, a tray table, and the bulky bed with its sit-up-or-lie-back mechanisms and bars on either side, there was barely space to move. Andy made himself small in a plastic chair, crammed between bed and curtain, while I took off my clothes and put on a gown. I heard him make a funny noise and turned around to find him sobbing, his face in his hands.

"Oh, sweetie, it's all right." Startled by the sudden forceful response, I stroked his shoulder. "I'm going to be fine. They'll take care of me here."

"I … I'm so sorry," he gasped, reaching for a Kleenex from a box on the tray table. "I should be comforting *you*."

"You don't have to be sorry. I'm all right. I'm going to be all right."

"I know. It's just … you're my best friend, and I just can't imagine my life without you."

I didn't quite know why Andy was talking as if I were dying. I was protecting myself through denial: *I do not feel that I am dying or could die, therefore I am not and will not.* I was not yet aware that a clot could enter my heart and kill me silently, before anyone in a white coat or set of scrubs could rush to my aid.

I simply thought the stress of seeing me in the hospital was hitting him hard. I thought again how much easier it was to be the patient than the patient's partner. I would later realize that hypochondria had trained him for this role.

I did not know that when I had cancer, he researched my diagnosis and prognosis. I did not know that he would now look up pulmonary embolism. He understood that the information I received from doctors was all I could handle, bare bones though it usually was. For his own sake, he had to go searching. He had to know as much as possible.

I thought he would go home, make himself a sandwich, distract himself with sitcoms, come back for an hour or so that evening, and return home to get some sleep. I thought if he could relax away from my bedside, he would reassure himself: I was fine. I was safe where I was.

As if I could ever just kick back on the couch while he lay in a hospital bed.

Andy returned in time for a visit by a radiologist. In a grave tone, the doctor told us the basics of the procedure I would have in the morning. A filter made of thin metal prongs, like the mechanism of a tiny umbrella, would be inserted through the femoral artery in my right groin and placed in the inferior vena cava (IVC), the main blood vessel leading to the heart. Once the umbrella was opened, the IVC filter would catch clots that might break off from the DVT, preventing them from entering my lungs and heart. In a few months, I would undergo another procedure to have the device removed.

The doctor said I would be under conscious sedation, meaning I'd know what was happening, but I'd be super relaxed about it. I couldn't quite picture that. The light in the room was dim. At last, I was appropriately scared. Scared of the procedure and scared because my life was at risk until they inserted the filter. Apparently they didn't consider this an emergency, though it was urgent enough for them to schedule the filter insertion for the next morning. The radiologist mentioned no other options. He placed a consent form on my tray table. I glanced over the page and signed it.

Later, I would watch a true crime program in which a rapist who's confessing to the cops expresses reverence for his hunting knife with the short, razor-tip blade, the one he holds to women's throats or presses to their sides—and I would be startled to find myself thinking back on this doctor's description of the filter.

The doctor left, Andy kissed me goodnight, and the nurse turned off the overhead light. My roommate still slumbered heavily. I listened to her long, slow, leaden breathing.

I imagined the filter—the slender, closed mini-umbrella—snaking its way toward my heart. They would put it inside me. As deep as anyone had ever gone. That night, I believe Michael Swango lurked somewhere in my memory, skulking around the edges of my conscious thoughts the way he snuck through hospital wards with his syringes full of death. He represented the danger I felt in the very atmosphere of this place, where a doctor could come right up to my bedside and coolly inform me that an object would soon be inserted into my body.

Mixed up with the story of Swango and his lethal injections were my mother's dread of invasive tests and procedures, the surgery that weakened her heart, and the anger and terror that overwhelmed me after I went under the knife. All of it at a level just below awareness, feeding my fear. My mother had taught me by example to dread medicine. I didn't need to remember her just then; I had absorbed her lesson into my cells.

What I thought at the time was, *You shouldn't be so afraid. A doctor is going to save your life. Again.*

Morning, the day after my admission: no breakfast. I got carted off in my bed to radiology, to a small room with a large ultrasound screen, monitors, and bright-white lights. I was moved from the bed to a padded table beneath the screen.

A doctor—maybe thirty years old, with startled, startling blue eyes—asked if I understood the procedure he was about to perform, in a *You get this, right? I don't really have to explain this, right? You'll soon be drugged senseless anyway, right?* sort of way.

"You're going to insert a filter so that the clot in my leg doesn't break off and travel to my lungs or heart."

He stared at me with those eyes that were beginning to creep me out. "The clots have *already* traveled to your lungs."

"Oh." In the whirlwind of the previous day, this actually had not occurred to me. Of course. It was not coincidence that I had the DVT in my leg and emboli in my lungs simultaneously. At this point, the filter was intended to protect my lungs and heart from additional clots that might break off from the DVT.

Like a small animal, I kept very still, as if I might blend into the background. I took shallow breaths. A nurse shaved the pubic hair around my right groin with an electric razor that tickled. She did the other side, too, which was nice; medically unnecessary, but cosmetically thoughtful. I was relieved when she covered the area with a surgical drape. Otherwise, the creepy-eyed radiologist would have been in a prime position to admire my newly trimmed pubis.

Another nurse started an IV. "My name is Mary. I'm going to be right here. If you need more meds, just say, 'Mary.' They come through your IV. You're getting Fentanyl and Versed. OK, Marcia?"

Fitting that the nurse should have been named Mary, because conscious sedation sure as hell seemed like heaven on earth.

The euphoria of Fentanyl, an opioid variably described as fifty to one hundred times more powerful than morphine, rocketed through my bloodstream. Where Vicodin made me feel like a god, Fentanyl took me over with its own supernatural powers, made me feel like it could lift me from the table and fly me into the stratosphere. In fact, I didn't move an inch. Versed, a sedative in the benzodiazepine class, kept me still and compliant. No pesky questions for the doctor, no way to even think of questions at this altitude, no talking at all except for calling Mary's name; I think only once, before I felt the full effects of the chemical onslaught she originally put in the IV. The euphoria and the sedation meant that the doctor could make an incision in my groin, thread the catheter through my femoral artery, and then place the filter through the catheter into the inferior vena cava, and I was so la-di-da that I didn't care. I wasn't worried about my heart or lungs. I didn't mind that this weird doctor had opened me and inserted an object deep inside, pushed it to a place more secret than sex.

It certainly didn't occur to me that the filter would later seem like a weapon. That hearing about drugs like Rohypnol, a depressant and muscle relaxant used by rapists to impair women's coordination and cognitive functioning, would remind me of Fentanyl and Versed.

Either Mary or the radiologist told me, "You probably won't remember any of this." This was supposed to be a comforting thought: that recall of an important bodily experience would be forever lost to me. But the image of the procedure room crowded with machines, my supine viewpoint, the sight of the doctor with his hands at my groin, and the overwhelming force of drugs would remain in my conscious memory.

I might have expected a huge rush of anger after my release from the hospital. Something akin to my rage after the thyroid surgeries. But a much stranger process took me over. By now I was used to being overpowered. It was not a shock.

A doctor could shoot me up with Fentanyl and Versed to shrink my fear—for the drugs did not take away fear; they only compressed it so I couldn't find it as I lay still beneath gloved hands—in order to access the depths of my body. It felt right that God should take me over next. It didn't matter what I called my higher power. A force bigger than me. I could call that force Lord or Fentanyl or Doctor.

What did it matter so long as I bent or lay down for that which possessed me, made my will irrelevant?

There was what I wanted: to be left alone. And then there

was what I was told to want, what I consented to, what was actually done.

I settled on the name God. A manlike figure I could focus on, who might listen. Who might have been listening since I began praying before my thyroid surgeries. I was still here, after all. I got down on my knees and told God I was sorry for wanting too much. Sorry for my year of anger. In case I had almost caused my own death from pulmonary embolism by longing for the safety of marriage, having unseemly writing ambitions. Raging at the unfairness of life. Failing to accept my loss of control during cancer treatment.

I told myself God was not the old man in the sky, yet I called him Him. A power greater than me was usually a male power. I willingly handed myself over to Him. I knelt for Him in a kind of anguished ecstasy. As I had handed myself over to the doctor who was master of my femoral artery, who drove an object through my groin and stopped just short of my heart. I had been immobilized by his drugs that thrust their way into my animal being, tying off both fight and flight.

I was high on life. High on the terror of being brought to what felt like the edge of existence. The previously unimaginable place where my mind flew even as my body was trapped, where being cut and entered meant being saved. The place that, when I recalled it now, felt just on the other side of death. Where the doctor brought me in order to preserve my life.

I had consented to the IVC filter, I reminded myself; I had signed the papers. Yes, I had been traumatized. But I had agreed to it. Wanting to live meant letting him do it.

I thanked God for allowing me to breathe, to creep back into my little life as if nothing remarkable had occurred.

Sometimes I thought the blood clots were the best thing that ever happened to me. Now I knew what my existence meant: it meant everything. It was rich and full, and I had no regrets. How lucky I was! That was what I couldn't get over. The bitterness, the

rage at the world of medicine I had experienced after cancer—
none of it came back. My life, long and prosperous, stretched
out before me. How many times since the hospital had I bowed
my head while sitting at my desk, weeping or just placing my
hand over my heart: *Thank you. Thank you for all of this.*

I knew now that I could survive any difficulty.

Though the lizard underbelly of gratitude was terror.

I found myself fantasizing about filling my handbag with
syringes, gauze bandages, alcohol swabs, a thermometer, a blood
pressure cuff. Dressing in the pale blue hospital gown, blue-and-
white-pinstriped robe, green socks with white rubber treads.
Stalking the streets and the halls at my temp job, riding the city
bus, entering restaurants, decked out in my patient uniform,
dragging my homemade medic's bag.

Wouldn't I feel safer if I could carry everything with me?
Would I even need doctors? What if they never invaded me
again?

Then there was my growing preoccupation with death.

I wrote cool meditations on the topic. Page after page:
Funny how I'd obsessed over suicide countless times over two
decades, and now I wanted nothing more than to live. A case of
be careful what you wish for. Just hilarious.

Youth, health, fun; jobs, bills; illness, middle age, old age,
retirement; happiness, misery; life: All temporary. Ha ha.

Soon after my hospitalization for blood clots, I was back to rail-
ing in my journals against Andy's disinterest in marriage. Yes,
he'd proven his commitment, his love, by staying at my bedside.
Still, I was desperate *to get married before one of us dies … Don't
leave me an unmarried widow. No status,* I implored him on pages
he would never read.

But we both knew—didn't we?—that I would go first. It was
looking that way. The law considered us total strangers. I could

not peacefully leave a world that did not recognize our love. And I wanted just one of my dreams to come true before my demise. I might never own a home, build a thriving editing business, or publish a book. It seemed inevitable that illness would continue to disrupt any hope of such stability. I would leave little behind. At least I could depart the world as Andy's wife.

Chapter 10

Broken

Nearly seven months after my IVC filter was placed, I was scheduled to have it removed. I was working at what would be my last job before turning to editing full-time. The economy was tanking. Temp assignments dried up. My editing clients, worried about their own finances, disappeared; for how long, I couldn't possibly predict. I knew I was fortunate, though I didn't feel that way, when Barnes and Noble hired me as a permanent employee that September, right before instituting a hiring freeze that would stay in place for many months.

Knowing I had grasped the security of full-time work just in time did not mitigate my self-pity. Despite all the challenges I'd faced since grad school, I still believed I should have been a published author by now. Instead, at thirty-seven, I was selling other people's books, earning barely more than minimum wage. I came home literally boo-hooing, as if I had been doomed to retail by the vocational gods.

I was not in the best frame of mind, then, when Andy and I went back to radiology to get the filter removed. I was under the impression that it would come out the way it had gone in: through the femoral artery. No one had said otherwise. There was some tiny measure of comfort in knowing what to expect. The Fentanyl, the Versed, not caring about the doctor at my groin.

I lay on a gurney in a room packed with gurneys, Andy crammed in beside me on a metal folding chair, both of us exhausted for another early-morning procedure. I recall no colors, just washes of gray.

A tall, skinny radiologist came by, scribbling notes, barely looking at me. He said something about my neck. Laid a gloved finger along the right side, above my thyroidectomy scar. I jumped. He didn't move his hand. I heard him say "jugular vein."

I panicked. "What do you mean, jugular vein? What about the femoral artery?"

The radiologist finally made eye contact with me. He removed his hand. He was frowning. "We don't take it *out* through the femoral artery," he said irritably. "We take it out through the jugular vein. In your neck."

Anger and terror closed my throat. I couldn't talk.

Andy does not normally speak for me, but this time, he had to. "Doctor, Marcia wasn't told this. She thought it would come out the way it went in. And she's scared about any incision in her neck." When the radiologist blinked at him, saying nothing, as if he hadn't noticed my faded scar, Andy dropped his polite tone, adding, "Because of her thyroidectomy. She had cancer. Don't you have her history?"

Also, we humans have a saying: going for the jugular. It means intending to really fuck someone up.

The radiologist blinked again. He turned to me. "Want some Valium?"

Oh, sure. I was inconveniently alert, with the gall to ask about which body part I was being expected to offer up. *Valium.* I was furious that he had no empathy to give, only drugs, and furious that the only drug he thought to offer was Valium. I'd taken much stronger sedatives. When my fear ramped up, I needed something more than the mother's little helper of the '70s. "All right," I managed to say.

As soon as he left, I whispered to Andy, "Valium is for *amateurs*. Valium won't do a damned thing." I shut up when I saw how worried he looked. He knew my anger was justified, but how would this go if I got too worked up?

For the sake of Andy's peace of mind and my own neck, I tried to calm down.

A nurse started an IV, which I would need for the Fentanyl and Versed, and injected the Valium. I'd completely forgotten the effects of Valium by IV before my thyroid surgeries.

"This will do not a single fucking thing," I couldn't help saying to Andy one last time after the nurse was out of earshot. A few minutes later, "I'm just going to lie back for a little bit."

Sometime after that, Andy was shaking me awake. "They're ready for you, honey."

Again I was told I wouldn't remember what happened while I was under conscious sedation. Again they were wrong.

I was fantastically high once more: It seemed as if the room with its glaring, white-hot lights were flying miles above the surface of the earth. My mind was sharp and fast, as if the old, slow one had been discarded. My body glowed beneath my skin as I lay in an exquisite stillness. I couldn't tell whether I was incapable of moving or just didn't want to move.

I lay on my left side, feeling the radiologist—a beefy guy, not the skinny doc who gave me the Valium—tugging at the right side of my neck. He was pulling the IVC filter out. I couldn't see what he was doing. There was some big machine over me, a giant, hovering black shape; I would later figure out that this was an ultrasound screen, showing the doctor exactly where my filter was. He was using a guidewire to hook the thing and drag it out.

Meanwhile, I was busy making plans in my head: Law school, just to prove how smart I was. Or a master's in social work, to help people, whom I suddenly loved *so much*. No, I'd get both—the law degree and the master's, because this mind could do it all.

"Goddamn it," the radiologist said. I was far too euphoric to be worried. The fact that something was wrong simply made me curious. "It broke," the radiologist said to the tech. She didn't say anything in return. He didn't say anything to me; I was drugged senseless, or so he thought. *Something broke. How interesting.*

The doctor finally pulled the last of the filter out of my neck. I felt no pain, just pressure. The tech swabbed my incision, put a bandage on it, and said, "You're done." Machines got wheeled out of the way with clicks and beeps and tubes being wound up, and I saw how huge this room was for just three people. They started to wheel me out, and I realized I could talk, now that the tugging was over.

"What happened? It broke?" I asked the tech. She looked away. The radiologist came to the foot of the gurney.

"One of the struts broke off," the radiologist said, looming over me. God, what was he, seven feet tall? A red-faced giant dressed in baby blue.

"Wow, really? What?"

"A *strut* broke off," the doctor said, more loudly this time. "A piece of the filter."

"Wow. Really?"

"I had a hell of a time getting the rest of the filter out," he said. We were just two people talking. Or like the mechanic talking to the car whose engine he just overhauled. "You want to see it?" he asked.

"Yeah!"

He held out his hand. In his palm was the little metal thing, the underpinnings of the miniature umbrella. It was smeared with blood, but there was no clot trapped inside. I didn't see the missing part.

"Wow." I wanted to ask if I could keep it, but even drugged, I knew this was a weird request.

"We have to send it off to see if it's defective," he explained, as if he knew I wanted to take it home.

The tech rolled me out, down the hall, toward the elevator that would bring us to the post-anesthesia care unit.

Later, when I'd sobered up, I learned to my horror that the strut was still in there, stuck in the wall of my inferior vena cava. Later still, when they did a scan, I was told that the two-inch-long strut was "fixed and embedded." Surgery to retrieve it would be too dangerous. And probably not necessary. Fixed and embedded. The thing wasn't going anywhere. Probably.

They never told me how close it is to my heart. I've never asked. I don't want to know. I've already pictured this piece of metal working its way out of the vessel wall and riding my bloodstream straight into my right atrium. Sometimes, when I'm practicing a forward bend from the waist during yoga, I imagine the strut breaking jaggedly, one half piercing the vessel all the way through. I don't know that these thoughts are entirely rational, but then no one ever explained how to approach living with a foreign object stuck inside my body.

I didn't, and don't, blame the radiologist for the filter breaking. Still, my heart rate speeds up when I recall how tall and brutally built he looked as I lay on my side—and when I remember his anger. I know he didn't injure me, but it feels as if he did. It feels as if he broke me. At least incisions heal and fade according to the body's natural responses to injury. This little piece of metal is unnatural, something that will forever be wrong in me.

When I think of the strut, I go very still. I offer a silent apology to my body. I send out a wordless prayer.

If anyone is to blame, it's the manufacturer who convinced

doctors that their crazy-looking product was a great idea. I don't know if anyone ever officially determined that my filter was defective; there was no mention of the issue in the medical records later sent to me upon my request. I'll just go out on a limb and say that it *was* defective, given that I will wear a piece of it indefinitely. In the years since my filter broke, I've seen countless TV ads by law firms representing patients whose IVC filters caused injury or "even *DEATH!*" but I don't have the fire in the belly needed to take legal action against the manufacturer.

In the immediate aftermath of the retrieval, my anger, like the strut, was fixed, embedded. It would find ways other than litigation to make itself known.

Late one night, I wrote a poem, undated but appearing on a page torn out of a college-ruled notebook I used as a journal during the months immediately preceding and following my IVC filter removal. I titled it "That Night." The setting is a deserted highway in 1975. The speaker is a man who has just sexually assaulted and killed a woman:

> How am I different
> from the surgeon? Tell me he does not enjoy
> cutting the flesh of a silenced woman, the feel of the blade
>   in his hand, the sight of
> the skin parting, the blood, the oozing viscera.
> Tell me he does not live for this,
> that he does not feel like a god,
> knowing he could take life as easily as he can save it.
> Tell me he does not feel kindness or sadness
> at the very same instant when he feels the thrill.

The next day, I stared at the page as if someone else had composed these lines.

Never have I been so stunned by the content of my writing. I hadn't yet started my late-night TV binges. I was years away from consciously connecting my surgeries to violent crimes. I had envisioned a character, his intimate thoughts, and his evil acts, all in one sitting. The poem isn't scrawled crazily in cursive. It is neatly, methodically printed, with almost nothing crossed out or inserted. As if it had dwelled in me for a long time, and chose this moment to make itself known.

This resembled no crime-drama plot I could recall. It did not come from my mother's true crime tales. I can see now that the story was suggested by a real murderer. I think he must be Ted Bundy, that intelligent killer who took up residence in my teenaged mind and never left. At fifteen, I was as obsessed with rock stars as my mother was with movie actresses, studying photo spreads in *Rolling Stone* while she read every word of the tabloid *Star*. I was enamored with U2's Bono and with John Lennon, whose murder only intensified his posthumous charisma. I was too afraid of Bundy to fall in love with him, especially after watching *The Deliberate Stranger*, but I couldn't help but be impressed by his fame.

I believe now that I was working it all out on the page, trying to rid myself of Bundy's presence nearly two decades after his execution, and either just before or just after I was scheduled to face another radiologist, another round of overpowering drugs, another guidewire snaking through me.

At the time I wrote the poem, and when I read it the next day, I wasn't consciously thinking of Bundy or the IVC procedure. But I couldn't squirm away from the fact that I'd compared sweet old Dr. Sixtysomething to a rapist-killer, as if he stood in for all doctors who had or would perform invasive treatments— my thyroid surgeries were the origin story of my medical dread. Rationally, of course, there was no comparison. There was no real link between the pretend murder victim and me. Between her silence and mine. Sure, I'd *felt* invaded by the thyroid surgeries. But Jesus. The old guy didn't try to kill me. He saved my life.

This was just some sick bit of literary play, I told myself. I thought I had made a game out of exploring a horrifying topic. I thought I had been monstrously unfair to my jolly-grandpa doctor. I felt guilty toward murdered women everywhere.

These were old fears amplified in an overheated mind, a mind stressed by further medical procedures. That was all this meant.

Whatever its artistic shortcomings, the murder poem is a vivid illustration of my growing interest in death. Not in meditations on death, but visions of actual death.

In journals from the months after I learned that I would permanently wear a piece of metal in the main vein leading to my heart, I find entries like this one: *I am settling into the idea of death more and more—my own, that is … It's because I'm tired, physically, emotionally, and spiritually.* It wasn't suicidal thinking; I wasn't depressed. It was the strong suspicion that the next medical crisis would kill me.

I realized that with no marriage on the horizon, I had to be pragmatic. I noted that I ought to draw up a will, so that Andy would get my books and my laptop and the rights to my work, published and unpublished; things of little monetary value, but things I thought he would want, and that I wanted him to have. I planned to get life insurance as soon as I could afford it, enough to cover my credit card debts and leave a cushion so that Andy could go on without me. I knew I couldn't tell him about the will or the life insurance. He'd understandably freak out. I also couldn't tell him I wanted nothing more to do with doctors.

Since I couldn't avoid it completely, I would minimize my contact with the world of medicine. I would only go to appointments *I* considered necessary. I would hope that no new diseases came to light.

I don't want life to end. I want medicine to end.

Chapter 11

Mercy

I began watching true crime in much the same way I watch it now: alone on the living-room couch, late at night, my books forgotten, with Andy reading in bed upstairs.

Almost exactly one year after the blood clot filter broke, I happened across an episode of *Forensic Files*, a show I'd never seen before. I figured if it was about forensics, it would focus on the science of investigation, and wouldn't display bloodshed, so it seemed safe to watch. I was right about the focus on science, and would later realize I was quite wrong about the bloodshed, but this particular episode had no gore—the victim had survived to tell her story. I found myself listening intently as a heavy-set woman in a bright red sweater described the neurological problems she'd suffered since her husband, a doctor, poisoned her with arsenic. Experts could hardly believe she was still alive, given the extremely high levels of the substance found in her hair samples.

The bizarre story, the woman's dignity as she discussed her ordeal, and the fact that the would-be killer was a doctor guaranteed that I would sit in rapt attention for the full half hour. *Mom would have loved this*, I wrote in my journal.

A few nights after the *Forensic Files* episode, I recorded this: *Am crying now over* 48 Hours Mystery, *a little girl testifying against her attacker. Like meeting people in grief. Like meeting spirits in death … Would it be lovely to be dead? Or just nothing?*

I also wrote of watching *Law & Order: Special Victims Unit*, which I had once strenuously avoided, all about rape and child molestation.

I was not disturbed by my new interest in these programs. The real stories offered satisfaction: The poisoning doctor gets caught. The little girl has her day in court. I cried for her and for myself, meeting her in grief for her lost innocence and for my own. My old belief that I would not want to survive being sexually assaulted was clearly still here; I was not watching a murder case, but after identifying with a violated girl, I quickly segued into fantasies of death.

Yet I saw another way on *Law & Order*. I saw women and children surviving rape. Whether or not justice prevailed, life went on.

I was not yet troubled by the idea that I was turning into my mother. I wasn't at the point of losing myself in mass-market paperbacks with images of bloody fingerprints and skeletal trees under darkening skies. I was just stumbling across these things on TV—shows that mostly didn't exist in the 1980s. I made a distinction between my mother reading her six-hundred-page books and me dipping into crime one hour at a time.

I had been through dark things. Death things. Cancer. Surgeries. A piece of metal stuck in my body. The anguished vulnerability that lingered after procedures made me feel death's nearness more sharply than did the diseases themselves. It was natural that I would seek out darkness. My mother had endured dark, death things, so many painful tests and treatments that after a while, all she read was darkness.

So my diseases and their treatments explained my fascination with death. But they didn't explain why I was particularly interested in stories about male perpetrators and female victims.

I had been repeatedly physically invaded. I was scared of doctors. I knew these things were connected in my mind. I thought I shouldn't connect them. The doctors who had performed my procedures were all men. But they hadn't meant to hurt me. It was shameful—crazy—to equate them with sadistic criminals, as I had done in my poem.

My doctors' intentions meant everything.

No one intended to harm me, therefore my medical procedures weren't really attacks. God, even thinking the word "attack"—it was ridiculous. I could not pretend to know what real victims of violence endured.

I didn't know why I was powerfully drawn to stories of sexual assault, a topic I had been unable to tolerate until now. I thought this must be part of my overreaction to medical treatment. The surgeon, the radiologists—none of them had said or done anything sexually inappropriate.

I didn't consider how they had overpowered me with drugs and entered my body; I forgot about how furious I felt long after the treatments were over. I didn't acknowledge that I felt violated by the doctors' blades and guidewires. I focused on how I had given my permission for these procedures, and in my mind, that meant I couldn't have been violated. I didn't think about the fact that I had agreed to these treatments under duress, that my life would have been at risk if I said no. I didn't ponder the fact that doctors held the power of life and death in their hands, the way a killer had the power to murder his victim or spare her.

I only knew that something in me could only be satisfied with stories of violation and images of death in the darkened living room.

Late at night, I wrote over and over in journal entries: *I'm in love with death!*

Each time I wrote it, I was stunned to read it the next day. Confused. I wasn't suicidal. This made no sense.

When I found hours of true and fictional crime programming lined up into the early morning, I felt happy. Appalled that I felt happy. I was relieved that I would be left alone in the dark, to watch as long as I wanted. I could no longer claim that I just happened to find these programs while channel surfing. By now, I was hunting for them.

I wrote in my journal about an MSNBC documentary on Elisabeth Fritzl, an Austrian girl kept for twenty-four years as a sex slave by her father, Josef Fritzl, in the basement of his home. She gave birth to seven of his children. On this particular night, I switched off my empathy for victims and joined the perpetrators' team. The winning team. The father was *quite fascinating;* his crime *very well-planned, brilliantly evil.* I offered no grief for his daughter.

It's obvious to me now why I identified with the father and not Elisabeth: I had not yet accepted how much my father's sexual interest had damaged me. If I didn't look too closely at the extreme suffering of this daughter, I could continue to minimize the pain of my experience; I didn't have to remember fearing that my father would enter my bedroom. Instead I focused on Josef's dungeon, how planning something so evil took discipline, a quality my father lacked.

I wrote that I thought I wanted to see violence done to other people because it spared me somehow. But then I allowed myself a rare, unvarnished acknowledgment—that I had experienced medical procedures as physical attacks: *Assault of Medicine. I won't go through THAT again. If I get cancer again, I'll willingly die of it.*

Here, in this journal entry, if nowhere else, the procedures counted as real violence. For once, I wasn't accusing myself of overreacting. I chose death by cancer over further medical invasions.

On an afternoon when Andy was away recording with his band, I found the Investigation Discovery network: true crime, 24-7.

Sometimes men were murder victims, too. But it wasn't the men I was looking for.

Damsels distressed by stalkers, molesters, sadists. Missing women found. Missing women lost forever. Lots of stylized reenactments, showing the act of murder, stopping short of portraying rape. Family members interviewed about their catastrophic losses. Crime scene recreations mostly taking the place of photos.

Yes. Yes. My terrible need answered, my feeble resistance quickly overpowered.

The stories were so similar, the criminals so alike in their annihilating vision, that the narration seemed to run together, creating one long tale of ruin.

Nothing much ever happened in this small town, until that night.

In the winter chill of our drafty, white-walled living room, I nestled against the generous cushions of the beige sofa, whose maternal appeal resembled that of the sofa in my therapist's waiting room. The old-fashioned box TV was a thirteen-inch eye onto every possible way of hurting every kind of woman.

Even seasoned detectives were horrified by what they saw.

Wrapping my arms around my knees, I stared at the screen, my heart quickening, my shelves full of books forgotten, my thirty-by-thirty-inch painting of ice-blue daubs on white above the TV fading from view.

The number of stab wounds indicated a personal connection to the victim.

Maybe the occasional neighbor passed by my kitchen window on her way from the carport to her condo; I didn't notice.

Sunny skies outside the sliding glass doors faded hour by hour into the late indigo afternoon. I don't remember getting up to eat or use the bathroom. The details of death and investigation mesmerized me.

A lock pick was found in his gym bag. In interrogation, the suspect looked like the boy next door. Like the devil.

Family members and friends who mourned the dead on camera told another story. Mothers were careful to preserve their daughters' memories.

She dreamed of being a model. A songwriter. A stay-at-home mom. I kept her room just the way it was the day she left.

Women recalled their dead sisters' selflessness.

She'd do anything for her kids.

Friends insisted, *She always had a smile on her face.*

Fathers choked up as they remembered the trials. *I told the judge it was a loss we almost couldn't bear.*

Narrators summarized the grief of everyone affected by murder and noted the remorselessness of killers. *Her parents wept as the guilty verdict was read. The defendant sat expressionless. His mother begged the court for leniency. Her parents laid white roses on her grave.*

Over and over, I saw the death of beauty: the smiling, rosy faces of actual victims, looking in portraits the way their families wanted to remember them.

I saw the eroticization of rape and murder: actresses playing corpses, lying face down and nude on beds, in open fields, in the woods. I saw it and I did not turn away.

I watched ID nonstop for six hours, until Andy came home that evening.

"Hey honey! How'd it go?" I said brightly, switching the channel.

"Great!" He wrestled his guitar case inside out of the cold. "The guys did really well. So, what have you been doing all day?"

"Um … I found this channel. Investigation Discovery. It's all crime."

"Oh, yeah? Like mysteries?"

"Not really. Like … *crime*."

He turned up the gas heater, as I had neglected to do. "Aren't you freezing in here?" he said. I was, I just hadn't realized it. "Why are you so sheepish about watching TV all day?" he said. "You work hard, all the time. Don't you think you deserve a break once in a while?"

I wanted to tell him about the specific stories I'd seen, but I couldn't. "It's just that it was pretty dark stuff."

"Well, we're all interested in dark stuff." Andy shrugged, hanging up his coat. "Some people won't admit it, but they're interested, too, believe me."

"They must be. This is a whole channel devoted mostly to … murder." I figured I had to make clear I wasn't talking about bank robberies where nobody got hurt.

"See? There you go. It's not like somebody invented a whole channel just for you."

No. It just felt that way.

For six months after I first found ID, every time I turned to the network, I found myself sitting for three, four, five hours or more. Looking for dead women. Watching whenever Andy was away at a gig or reading upstairs in bed so he wouldn't realize I'd become a sicko. Waiting for commercial breaks to eat or use the bathroom so I wouldn't miss a single detail.

During those months, I had little understanding of my obsession, except I could no longer deny that it resembled my mother's. I could see why she needed to relate the bizarre stories she read about; I badly wanted to tell Andy the details of what I was watching. Yet I knew that my obsession didn't stem entirely from my mother's tales. It had to do with medicine's invasions, but it wasn't all about exploring death either. Death by natural causes didn't interest me. Medical dramas didn't appeal to me. Only violent death captured my attention, as it had captured my mother's.

I realize now, I resisted the idea that I had been violated not so much because I didn't want to accuse doctors of hurting me, but because I didn't want the shame of knowing I had allowed intimate parts of my body to be invaded by men. The shows I watched frequently implied that women were at least partly to blame for domestic violence, stalking, rape, and murder. They were irresistibly beautiful. They were friendly to strangers. They left their windows unlocked. They jogged alone at night. They let men get them drunk. They went back to abusive partners. If women were responsible for their terrible fates, TV viewers could be less outraged on behalf of victims, and more interested in how the abusers, stalkers, rapists, and murderers succeeded in punishing women for their mistakes.

I wasn't interested in expressing my feelings about medicine through healthy, therapeutic methods. Ranting in my journal. Using boxing moves during at-home dance aerobics sessions. Pounding pillows. Some would have said that active expression would be more effective than sitting on the couch, transfixed by images of blood-soaked crime scenes, both recreations and photos—bloody puddles in bathtubs, blood spatter on white walls, blood-streaked kitchen knives, bloody footprints made by bare feet on kitchen tiles, blood halos around the heads of gunshot victims, blood lakes in the center of mattresses—

No. Nothing that was healthy could possibly compare to all the crimson, ruby, and garnet my eyes drank in. Journaling, boxing moves, and pillow pounding sounded right because they were physical. But they weren't real violence. They didn't address anger and fear. True crime laid a cold finger on my heart, saying, *I know you. I know what you know.*

Once, the stories of sexual violation followed by murder would have given me nightmares. Now, I watched them, brushed my teeth, turned out the lights downstairs, and trotted up the dim staircase to bed.

As if what I had long feared had already happened to me.

But in reality, the only person who ever intentionally hurt me was me. I was the perpetrator and the victim of attempted self-murder. I understood something of the murderer's urgent, physical need to annihilate. I had felt violent impulses course through my body.

I could not claim that an overdose is not violence.

I saw a lot of poisonings in the true crime shows. They require planning, stealth, and determination. As did my suicide attempt at age twenty-seven. A few days before, I had talked the pharmacist into an early refill of my medication so I'd have what I believed to be a lethal dose. I gave no one any reason to suspect my intentions. I chose an early hour, just after dawn, when I knew my roommate would not be up. I closed my door so that if she did get up, she would think I was still asleep, and wouldn't disturb me until it was too late to intervene.

The poisoner is in some ways a more chilling figure than the shooter or knife-wielder. Hers is no crime of passion but a methodical, deliberate act.

I have to live with the fact that on that July morning in 1998, when I shoved thirty-three capsules into my mouth, I had no mercy. Maybe my change of heart an hour later was mercy of a sort: I didn't want to suffer pain. But I had expected to die within that hour. I left a note addressed to family and friends. I took the drugs with food so that I would be less likely to throw them up.

The time it took to chew bread with peanut butter, to swallow so many capsules. It must have taken at least fifteen minutes.

Then that hour, waiting for consciousness to dim, and go black.

I believed I ought to die. I waited for it to happen.

Seventy-five minutes without mercy.
It wasn't the surgeon I should fear most.

Chapter 12

The Surgeon and the Mugger

The year after I began watching true crime brought major changes. In the spring, I was finally able to leave Barnes and Noble and support myself entirely through editing. It marked the beginning of the writing life I had long envisioned.

In the fall, Andy's mother died after a relatively short battle with dementia.

Having spent two years looking after his mother during her rapid decline, Andy now turned his caretaking attentions back to me. He was terribly worried about my neglect of my dental health and its implications for my overall health. Now, with his inheritance and my newfound earning power, we could afford to have me catch up.

I knew he was right. I hadn't had regular dental care since my early twenties. But I couldn't stop superimposing medicine's threats over the comparatively simple practice of dentistry. Drill now meant whining knife-point power tool. I saw biopsy needles thrust over hours into the tender red of my gums.

I was going to need drugs.

I would undergo two rounds of intensive treatment with two different dentists, both men. The first gave Fentanyl and Versed orally; the second administered the same drugs through IV. On each visit, the drugs failed. They surged in my veins like a strong but fleeting emotion. I was astonished by the despair that swept through me in their wake. It was the despair which stilled me, that and the fear of the shrieking drill.

I agreed to wear a black mask over my eyes, which the dentists said allowed many patients to sleep while they worked. I knew I would not sleep, but I thought it would help if I couldn't see the instruments. I didn't realize that taking off the mask once the sedation failed would have allowed me the most basic form of communication with the dentists and hygienists. As long as I wore the mask, they had no way of knowing how I felt. With a prop in my mouth to keep it open, I could only groan an approximation of "Uh-huh" when they asked if I was doing OK. I could have shaken my head or struggled to free my hand from the black nylon drape to indicate that I needed a break, but I didn't dare stop them. I needed this to be over.

Sometimes the mask slipped, and I saw all the hot white lights and gleaming silver sharps. I saw the clock on the wall. What I didn't see were eyes.

On both occasions, I spent many hours in the chair. The first time, I hadn't realized that extracting a tooth meant drilling it until it split in two, and then rocking each half back and forth like a fence post until it came free. I didn't recall that fillings were pressed in hard by hand, that having my jaw held by strong fingers would leave me voiceless even after they let go, even after the prop was removed from my mouth.

There was nothing to say after being so thoroughly controlled.

A few months after the first dental appointment, I was hit with a savage bout of depression that lasted for twelve weeks, unusually long for me. At the time, I attributed it entirely to business trouble. Editing work had dried up, for reasons I could never discern. The timing of the onset makes me suspicious now. I wonder if my psyche was weakened enough by those hours in the dentist's chair to let depression in after years without an episode.

Depression is not the smothering softness the term implies, but the gleaming blade that guts the self. I felt wholly inadequate to the task of living. Afterward, I managed to incubate an embryotic version of myself. Client emails began flooding my inbox as abruptly as they had vanished three months earlier. In reply, I pretended to be a whole person until I was one again. It was my fifteenth episode. My sixteenth birth.

I avoided dentistry for a full year. I had chronic dry mouth, which put me at high risk for developing more cavities; I was told I needed cleanings and exams three to four times per year, but I simply couldn't face the prospect of going that often, as each visit would remind me of those long hours in the chair. I had promised Andy I would return at some point when I was ready, and pushing that thought from my mind created an undercurrent of tension.

I went to work, driven by that undercurrent.

Unable to write even after I recovered from depression, I turned to another familiar outlet, painting acrylic abstracts. I mostly didn't plan the images; I waited to see what emerged. What a relief, to stop planning. To stop trying for the perfect sentence. To lose control. To express the visceral instead of the carefully considered thought.

I bought many shades of red. When I used one, I immediately regretted the choice, and muted it or covered it altogether with some other color. Underneath my nice bright yellows and blues, I often left slivers of brick and magenta, the little cuts I could live with. Sometimes I left flurries of smudged crimson thumbprints where they were, as long as they looked vaguely like scattered petals, or the vestiges of paw prints marking a scurry to safety.

I loved using the palette knife to apply paint, scraping and slicing and smearing, sometimes almost piercing the canvas, in a frenzy I interpreted as artistic passion.

My year of painting yielded about fifty canvases. I chose my favorites to hang in my home office. I sat at my desk, tapping out edits on clients' files, forgetting the images that surrounded me: Oxblood spatters and ochre eruptions. Black-and-blue galaxies, stars taking last gasps in red and yellow sparks. An inescapable mass of orange leaves without branch or trunk. A black diptych with crude white oblongs, bones or hammers or hammering bones. I didn't ask myself why these were my favorites. I believed I had chosen colors and forms and textures by instinct, a mysterious guiding force that originated in the belly, as if the brain were not involved.

One twelve-by-sixteen canvas, dark, thick matte blue partially lit up in green and white speckles, I had hung on its own slender section of white wall, between the closet and the door that opened to the rest of the house. Only when that door was closed did I glimpse the painting. Only later did I see it: it looked like a PET scan of the unconscious, the mind's watery depths.

Sometime after the second round of dental work, I began to switch the channel more often to *Forensic Files*.

In one episode, an aspiring model is sexually assaulted and murdered by a photographer. He dresses her body and buries her in sandy soil on the side of a mountain. Police pressure the killer repeatedly until he leads them to her grave. Nine days later, her body is perfectly preserved. Photos show a forensics team at work, digging. First, a pair of knees. Next, the entire body: the bare, still-pink flesh of her thighs, lightly dusted in gray sand; torso covered in a short white jumpsuit; knees and elbows bent as if she has curled up here to sleep. Her long, honey-colored hair spills over her shoulder, revealing a portion of her face: eyes closed, again as if sleeping.

Then I saw not rest, but death: a shot of the pinks, purples, and reds on the side of her face, indicating manual asphyxiation. Close-ups of bruising on her wrist, ligature marks on her ankles.

I took shameful, confused, immense comfort in her tucked-in pose, in her silence, in the beauty preserved and the savagery uncovered. I was not sure what I wanted, her rest or her death. A part of me that cried out without words was satisfied, spoken to, by both.

A few months after those hours in the second dentist's chair, I began to panic about returning for a scheduled cleaning. Mostly, I'd be with the hygienist, but the dentist would at some point enter the room and insert his gloved fingers into my mouth. Since I was at high risk for cavities, he might well find more.

Then all of it, again.

I had decided there was no point in having IV sedation the next time I needed cavities filled. I didn't know if nitrous oxide would help. I didn't know if anything could help me.

In the weeks before the appointment, I couldn't sleep. I had trouble focusing on work. I sobbed several times a day. Every nerve in my body hummed with fear as my mind hummed with the remembered shriek of the drill. But if I went back to ignoring my dental health, my teeth would start falling apart again.

Days before the appointment, I began vomiting while brushing.

Next stop: Vanessa, my therapist.

I described the problem. I'd told her about my previous dental troubles, but the vomiting was a new feature. Her face grew serious, then brightened. "I use self-hypnosis when I go to the dentist," she said in her sweet, soft, reasonable voice.

I stared at her, keeping my mouth shut. I don't want to

alienate the normal people. They're too hard to replace. Instead I screamed at her inside my head:

What? Self fucking hypnosis? Do I look like a candidate for this technique? Woman, I need DRUGS. And the drugs this dentist gave me last time didn't work. And even if they had, he wouldn't put me under for a cleaning—or he shouldn't.

Vanessa pulled a book from her shelf. *Discovering the Power of Self-Hypnosis.* Yeah, right. That didn't sound at all like something you'd see in an infomercial at three in the morning.

"You can borrow this if you like," she said.

I wanted to say: *I'm not like you. God, how I wish I were, but I'm not. After eight years, don't you know that stuff like this doesn't work on me? It depresses me that you don't know this.*

I took the book in my hands.

Maybe there was a sliver of a thread of a possibility that one chapter, one passage, even one line might somehow ease my fear.

Maybe.

"I'll try anything at this point," I said. Recalling that she was trying to help, and that she had helped me many times in eight years, I added, "Thank you."

At home, I showed the book to Andy.

"*You're* going to read *that?*"

I shrugged. "Maybe flip through. You never know."

I hate self-help books. I occasionally pick them up in bookstores, because who doesn't want to reclaim or renovate or reinvent their lives? Who wouldn't like to adopt a neat, simple plan of three or five or eight principles that will address every difficulty, every bad habit, every hang-up? I never get very far. I quickly zero in on the principle that sours the deal:

Screw forgiveness. Love myself—oh, like I never thought of that? Like I wouldn't be doing it already if I could?

I can't help noticing that this crap is mostly watered-down Eastern philosophy, set in a cognitive-behavioral framework that's much easier to fathom than those maddening Zen koans.

Suitably desperate, I settled in that evening with the work of Stanley Fisher, PhD, a psychologist and psychoanalyst. In Chapter One, I learned that hypnosis is not a magic trick, but a state of relaxation and focus. It sure sounded nice. Too bad it would never work on me. The title of Chapter Two caught my attention: "Self-Hypnosis in Preparation for Surgery." Why would hypnosis help if you were under anesthesia?

Early in his career, when he first began working with patients anxious about surgery, Fisher came across a *New York Times* article which discussed how people are prepared for the OR. They receive a sedative beforehand. Once they're on the table, they are given an anesthetic and a muscle relaxant to prevent the body from tensing. If you were unconscious, why would the body tense up during surgery?

The *Times* article gave Fisher a way to view his recent success in using self-hypnosis to prepare a very frightened, very skeptical patient for an emergency quadruple bypass. He had taught the patient to relax before, *during*, and after the procedure. What was he to make of this? Why had it worked?

One idea made sense to Fisher: that the body can't tell the difference "between a surgeon and a mugger."

I stared at that line.

"Oh, my God," I whispered, "oh, my God." I kept reading.

Fisher pointed out that "the body usually reacts to the scalpel as though it's a knife" in the hands of an assailant. I felt the truth of this in the very cells of my tingling flesh. I shivered as I stared first at "scalpel," then at "knife." I saw now that my body had indeed registered the scalpel as a dire threat, that it had not recognized the surgeon's benevolent intentions. I allowed myself to see what I had always known on some level: I sought out true crime programs because my body had experienced surgery as violence. The IVC filter insertion and retrieval, too. And the dental work. I wasn't crazy. I hadn't overreacted.

I wanted to weep with relief, but I was too stunned for tears.

I wanted to roll up this slender paperback, thrust it into the air like an Olympic torch and run with it—around my living room and out the door and down the street, shrieking—but I didn't move. Now I had the words I needed, and I didn't have to say them yet. Someone else had said them for me: *surgeon, mugger, knife, the body*. This psychologist understood me, and noted that there were many others like me. Finally, I wasn't alone with my true crime obsession and my terror of medicine. The shame I'd felt when I first saw my thyroidectomy scar made sense—it was the shame of the violated. *Violated*. I could use that word when I was ready.

There was more to it all, but this was what I understood that night in my living room.

What did all of this mean for my upcoming dental appointment? I had a few days to heal myself of six years of trauma. Even the overachieving-child part of me was dubious.

I began with a writing exercise, which the overachieving child was only too happy to complete. Dr. Fisher's book recommends pinpointing the problem you're struggling with and then imagining yourself free of the problem.

Thinking of the surgeon-as-mugger line, I asked myself what I feared most. I feared the cleaning not so much in itself, but because it might well lead to another appointment to fill cavities. Was the point of the drill any different from the point of a knife?

Under "My issue," I typed, *I am terrified of going to the dentist*. If I could be free of this problem? *I will feel grateful for my life*. Even in the privacy of my office, I couldn't bring myself to write the statement that had first come to mind: *I am terrified the dentist is going to kill me*.

But my quickened breathing and shaky fingers told me I'd nailed my problem to the wall, even if I was too embarrassed to record it. Not being murdered by a spinning sharp: that was my picture of success.

Next, I read Fisher's detailed instructions for self-hypnosis. I didn't think I could work my hypervigilant mind into a trance if I had months to practice and Fisher himself to talk me through it. Frantically flipping through the book for the crash course, I found that yoga and meditation could have much the same effect as self-hypnosis.

The simple yoga routines I'd practiced for a decade included a short meditation at the end. My brain kept nattering through the yoga moves and the final minute or so of stillness, though sometimes the narrative shifted from its usual recitation of anxieties to thoughts like "My body is letting go of tension. I think I hate myself a little less." Not exactly the state of deep relaxation Fisher was talking about.

A longer period of meditation might get me there. I might actually be able to gain control of my mind.

With one day left before the appointment, I headed to Barnes and Noble, my former workplace. Grabbing a copy of *Yoga Journal*, I thought it was kismet—or should I say karma?—that the issue contained an article on meditation. (I would later learn that the magazine almost always has an article on this topic.) In the music department, I scooped up three meditation CDs and a DVD. Laying it all on the glass counter, I recognized the cashier, a quiet guy I used to work with but never got to know well, a musician who had probably tried and failed to convince himself that this job was good for his creative life, as I had tried and failed to do.

"I'm kind of stressed out," I said as he eyed the stack of relaxation materials. "I think these will help."

"Cool," he said, running the handheld scanner over all the bar codes in that swift, methodical way I, too, had perfected.

A half hour later, I was home in my office, flat on my back on the yoga mat, a CD with the sounds of flutes and gongs piping into my headphones from the laptop. It was such sad music that I found myself beginning to surrender to it, breathing along with its desolate rhythms. Maybe this was depression's payoff, at long last: I knew how to give up if I was sad enough, and giving up was exactly what I needed to do now. My body seemed to matter less as I lay there.

I focused on a mantra to keep the chatter of *I'm scared of the drill, I want the REAL drugs, I can't go, I can't let them touch me again* turned down in the background of my thoughts, mixed up with the flutes and gongs.

That day, I went through four twenty-minute and two forty-minute meditation sessions, plus fifteen minutes of yoga.

I went to the dental appointment the next afternoon, after an hour-long meditation in the morning. I felt no panic upon leaving the house nor even after I stepped through the practice's door; I was surprised to realize that I only felt a manageable level of anxiety. When I confessed to being nervous, and asked the hygienist to explain what she was doing before she did it, and tell me immediately of any suspected cavities, she said, "I'll do anything to make you comfortable."

I'll do anything—I never knew how badly I wanted to hear that from a medical professional.

The dentist popped in briefly, long enough to confirm the hygienist's assessment that I had no cavities. I focused on taking long, deep breaths while he was in the room. Again, no panic, even in the presence of the guy with the drill. I could hardly believe meditation had helped me this much.

"I'm so happy you came back," he said.

I realized something I hadn't noticed before: he was shy, which I had mistaken for a lack of empathy.

I told Vanessa about my new insights, and my successful encounter with dentistry. I finally disclosed to her my TV viewing habits. I was afraid—even with this new insight—that she'd warn me off, saying a depressive shouldn't expose herself to stories of violence, images of death.

Instead, she was impressed by what I'd managed to put together, and glad that the book she suggested helped me in this most unexpected way.

"But why do I still want to watch this stuff, now that I understand what's behind it?" I asked.

She told me about a professional conference she had attended recently, where one of the speakers was an expert in treating psychological trauma. "He said that if someone has a phobia of sharks, you have them watch *Jaws*. And not just once. Over and over."

But Vanessa was not a trauma specialist, at least not the kind I'd heard about: therapists who hand you phone books to beat with rubber hoses, or teddy bears to throttle, or who goad you into long-overdue tantrums. Instead, she listened as I spoke of being terrified by medicine, describing procedures more graphically than I had before—the violence I experienced as my life was saved. She witnessed not only the facts of my invasions, but the story I made of them, fear threaded like a bright-blue ribbon through the weave of ordinary beige existence.

Often my voice trembled with fury, with grief suddenly unbound. I wanted her to get angry, hearing all of this. She rarely did. I think she did not see getting angry on my behalf as part of her job.

A slight, quiet woman heard me and did not turn from me. I am not sure I can ask for more, from anyone.

I considered the unconscious mind. I'd never given it much thought since learning the basics of Freudian theory in college psychology classes. But I did take note of Freudian slips, marveling at how the truth outs itself in the misspelled word, the check sent without a signature for a debt we don't want to pay.

My dreams often informed me that I was more worried about something than I'd admitted to.

But I didn't like that clunky term, *unconscious*. I didn't like the modern term for the actual part of the brain that's responsible for the unconscious processing of sensations, *limbic system*, coined in 1952 by neuroscientist Paul D. MacLean. Such unattractive words for such brilliant concepts.

I like taking language away from men and giving it my own twist. I called my unconscious "undermind": the ocean floor of my psyche where dark attaches to dark. When we say "the body remembers," we're really referring to the unconscious. Flesh doesn't have memory. But I came to realize that the undermind records everything that happens to us.

Slowly, now that I knew why I watched true crime, I would uncover the reasons why I specifically sought out stories of rape. Yes, I had experienced medicine as violence, but no doctor had abused me. What did rape have to do with me?

One day, I sat in the silence of my office with no Internet connection, the window closed on the sunny afternoon, my laptop power cord the only link to the present. Something about my childhood was pressing on me, some aspect of it wanted my recognition, as if it knew that I was ready to make connections between seemingly disparate experiences. Using nothing but electricity and memory, I began to discover the thread of fear that ran through my past. Over the next weeks, I tapped out page after page:

I dreamed Bigfoot was breaking into my bedroom window … Randy wanted to date my sister … My mother told me terrible stories … My father took too great an interest in my developing body.

I had never considered the cumulative impact of these events. I had never thought of them at the same time, and so I had never connected them. Finally, I appreciated how very anxious I'd been as a kid, how frightening my parents' drinking was, how I'd been taught to fear sexual threat inside and outside my home. I grew up expecting men to hurt me.

Around this time, I began to accept that my undermind had collected countless examples of sexual assault. Before medicine, I had consciously pushed away all knowledge of rape, but I couldn't erase it: my mother's stories, news stories, *Law & Order* plots gleaned in the seconds before I could turn the channel. About men with knives, ropes, gags. Men who slipped Rohypnol into women's drinks or targeted those already intoxicated. Men who killed by going for the throat. I realized that despite my efforts to quash them, these stories had always lived in me.

The full picture came to me image by image. I had to let go of rational comparisons. I had to remind myself I wasn't actually accusing physicians of abusing or trying to kill me.

On an episode of *Law & Order: Special Victims Unit,* a woman lies on an autopsy table as the medical examiner explains the cause of death to the cops. A rapist held a knife to the woman's throat, pressing with sufficient force to cut her inferior thyroid artery. She choked to death on her own blood.

I looked at the wound at the base of her throat and found myself nodding at the screen. The size and shape resembled my thyroidectomy incision when it was still healing. Instead of sinking again into fear and rage, I felt understood. I nodded in order to acknowledge that an image on TV reflected the scar no one thought I should be upset by.

In another *SVU* episode, a man forces a woman to engage in oral sodomy (we only hear the characters talking about it; thankfully, we don't see it). I thought about what it felt like to have instruments and fingers and props inserted in my mouth during dental work. I struggled with this one: *What, those dentists, those gentle men? Are you crazy?* Again, I had to remind myself—it wasn't about the dentists. It wasn't about actually being raped. It was about the feeling of being overpowered. Those instruments, those props had filled my mouth, silenced me for hours. I was even blindfolded, unable to communicate with my eyes.

I studied more images of rape and murder on TV. From *SVU* to ID's *Ice Cold Killers* to Lifetime docudramas, the setup is the same: A man stands over a woman he has pushed to the bed or the floor or the ground, weapon in hand. The way doctors and dentists stood over me as I lay prone, holding a scalpel or guidewire or drill. The contexts don't match, but the visuals do. I could see it so clearly now. I had never allowed myself to see it before.

I was stunned by an episode of *Forensic Files*, in which a doctor uses Versed to incapacitate a female patient before sexually assaulting her. I didn't know what it felt like to be raped, but I knew the experience of having my body taken from me while I was still conscious. I saw Versed and Fentanyl as physical and emotional assaults in and of themselves: The unnatural euphoria. The forced disconnection from flesh, from fear. The racing of the mind and the stillness of the body.

If my undermind didn't know the difference between a knife and a scalpel, a mugger and a surgeon, a cut meant to kill and one meant to save, I reasoned, perhaps it also didn't distinguish between a sexual assault and the insertion of a foreign object though an incision in the groin, between conscious sedation and date-rape drugs, between being silenced for benign purposes and being prevented from screaming for help.

Finally, I came to the realization that crystalized my understanding. The throat, the groin, the mouth: they are all erotic areas of the body.

The knife, appearing twice in rapid succession, cut away my longstanding dread of the rapist. Instead, the surgeon, and later the radiologists and the dentists, fulfilled the role of the terrifying male.

I was every woman whose boundaries have been transgressed by men, but knows her story doesn't count.

It's not violence if you sign your name.

It's not abuse if everyone is laughing.

Don't worry.

Don't talk. Don't move.

Do you know what happens to young girls? Do you know what men do?

Chapter 13

Survivors

I still go looking for dead women on true crime TV, thirteen years after the thyroid surgeries. I'm still working out what has happened to my body. I'm still drawn to the idea of death as the ultimate safety, as perfect rest. I've heard and seen stories of men murdering women all of my life. At first I was unable to shut them out. Later, I was unable to stop seeking them out.

The female corpse is a central image in the iconography of misogyny. Its power isn't easily reversed.

At the same time, I'm increasingly drawn to women who speak of surviving sexual assault. I am dumbstruck by Elizabeth Smart's poise and strength on camera as she describes the man who invaded her bedroom and kidnapped her by knifepoint when she was fourteen, the sexual and psychological abuse she endured during nine months of captivity. I read Alice Sebold's *Lucky*, which details the brutal rape she suffered as an eighteen-year-old college student and includes her astonishing trial testimony that put her assailant away, and I want to raise both fists in the air, as if her legal victory is mine. But it's not mine, and the moment of victory didn't magically heal Sebold, just as making connections between past and present transgressions of my body didn't magically heal me.

When I watch episodes about rape on Investigation Discovery programs, I lose myself, and take recreations as seriously as if they were news footage. I need to see the bogeyman get caught, over and over and over. He is the same man. He is my father and Randy and the rapists from my mother's stories. He is the stranger, the man who walked up to me on a crowded street in downtown Burlington and said in a low voice, with a criminal's utterly calm assurance, "I can see your breasts through your shirt," handing me the humiliation and fear I deserved for wearing a white tank top. I need to see the moment when the cops snap on the cuffs. I love it when survivors testify in court; I love it when the bad men get sent to prison. I really love it when a sniper's bullet kills a rapist-murderer, saves a cop, a woman, a child, all women, all children. No trial, no technicalities, no appeals. Safety. Silence.

One Christmas, a few years after my surgeon-mugger epiphany, Andy gave me a set of kitchen knives. Pretty brave of him, considering.

One was an extremely sharp paring knife, perfect for eviscerating apples. Another, less sharp but longer, with a serrated edge, became my go-to household implement; I used it for everything from chopping eggplant to opening Tyvek envelopes. The third, wide and flat, with a wicked point at the tip of its twelve-inch blade, was the one used in all the cooking shows. And all the true crime shows. It's Alex Forrester's weapon of choice in *Fatal Attraction,* Skyler White's in the third-to-last episode of *Breaking Bad.* Andy and I promptly christened it the Murder Knife.

I tried using it for its intended purpose, food preparation. It was so heavy, I couldn't chop vegetables with it unless I wanted to risk a repetitive motion injury. As a vegetarian, I didn't need it to lop off wings or heads. It lay neglected in the utensil drawer, glistening with untapped culinary and evil potential.

Well, I did find one use for it.

I had begun to get angry at male perpetrators of sexual violence against women. Fear had started to seep back in, too—not the heightened fear of my college days, but appropriate vigilance. I double-checked the locks on the doors and windows downstairs before heading up to bed. When Andy was out late at night, I waited until he came home before I undressed for the shower.

I thought of the Murder Knife. How it could be used not just for offense, but for defense.

Now, was I really going to brandish that thing and succeed in scaring off an intruder? I couldn't even manage to chop basil with it. What exactly was I going to do to a man who was bigger and stronger? Mince his guts out?

And it was all the way downstairs. Unless I slept with it under my pillow—and Andy would have had something to say about that—it was useless.

No, I couldn't truly picture myself using it in self-defense. I wasn't so afraid that I felt the need for a weapon.

A fantasy weapon: that was more my speed.

Very late at night, after watching yet another true crime or crime drama program in which a husband, a father, a boss, a stranger destroyed yet another woman's sense of safety in the world, I would think of the Murder Knife. I went to the kitchen drawer, grasped the heavy black hilt. Lifting my deadly Christmas gift, I lightly fingered its tip.

"If you touched me, I would kill you. *I would kill you*," I whispered to the knife.

"You" meant not the knife, but the men I'd seen on TV. It meant my father. The men were locked up. My father was dead. Still I gripped the handle so hard my hand trembled. I found myself breathing heavily. I didn't like this. I didn't like who I was with that knife. What would Andy think if he saw me, heard me? I replaced it carefully in the drawer. Until the next time I felt the need to talk to it again.

By now, I've stopped talking to the knife. I don't want to invite fear so far into my life that I feel the need to arm myself. It's been in the drawer since the last time I laid it down.

I feel guilty when people assume I've been through chemotherapy and radiation, and I'm obliged to admit that I haven't. I might be imagining it, but they always seem a little disappointed. Like they want to know they're talking to a brave cancer warrior, and I have nothing but this puny, faded scar to show them. I can't say I fought cancer. I lay there while stuff happened to me.

And I'm still afraid.

The scars left by medicine aren't just on my skin. The ones on my psyche are not ennobling. Sometimes they're embarrassing.

I have not had my hair cut by a professional since my surgeries, which occurred more than a decade ago. I still have this little hang-up about seeing a stranger come at me with a sharp object. I know, I could pick a woman stylist and go only to that person, develop a relationship, work on trusting her. One winter, I pondered this, and meanwhile my hair was getting out of control: a long, dark mass of split ends and tangles that made me dread the shower and the labor of lathering, rinsing, and drying. Finally, I asked Andy to trim the back and sides after I snipped the bangs. Andy liked the idea of this task, seeing it as sensual, "like that hair-washing scene in *Out of Africa,* but with scissors."

In our tiny half bath, with the door closed to keep out our inquisitive cat, I sat on a cold metal folding chair, an old towel wrapped around my shoulders. Andy stood very close behind me. There was almost no room for either of us to move. In the mirror over the sink, I saw the tension in my face.

Then Andy picked up the red-handled pair of shears.

"Ready?"

Andy is the person I trust most in the world, topping the severely abbreviated list of people I trust at all. I was all right while he worked on the tresses in the back. But when he came to my side and brought the blades close to my cheek, saying urgently, "Don't move," because he was determined to cut my straight hair straight, it was as if I forgot who he was. I felt the long, dull metal edge graze the side of my neck as Andy prepared to trim along my jawline. My breathing quickened. My heart rate spiked. Tears came to my eyes. When he accidentally pressed the tip of one blade against my throat, a few inches above the surgical scar, I gasped, startled but not actually hurt; it didn't leave even the suggestion of a scratch.

I realized that this whole setup put me not in a movie but right back in the thyroid surgeries. Mixed in somewhere was the creepy-eyed doctor inserting my IVC filter, and later, the filter breaking, the beefy radiologist tugging at the jugular vein in my neck like he was trying to reel in a big fish on a tangled line.

Finally, I confessed what I was feeling. Poor Andy, who was just trying to do a nice thing, learned that I was reacting to him as if he were a predator. Not surprisingly, it unnerved him, and I felt small and ridiculous and damaged.

I've trimmed my own hair since. Andy didn't want to relinquish the task even after I explained that my undermind registered him as just another guy with a knife. But I don't want to put him in the position of predator again, for his sake and for mine. Plus, I'm more daring with the cutting than Andy is—it's my head, after all. I chop off huge hunks until I've got a heap of dark fluff on the bathroom floor, as if a small, shaggy animal decided to crawl in and die right there on the linoleum. I go very short in minutes, and then I spend a good hour snipping a millimeter at a time, until something resembling a style emerges. Very short hair suits my face. And leaving nothing to hide behind is an act of aesthetic courage—much easier to come by than physical courage.

Andy likes the look, but still asks, "Wouldn't you rather pay someone to do this? It's an awful lot of work." I always shake my newly lightened head.

Hair styling, like medical treatment, is intimate. When I was younger, I enjoyed the salon pampering, but by now, I've had plenty of personal attention paid to my body; I don't care to go looking for more. When a stylist shrouds me in one of those black nylon drapes, I'm going to remember the dentistry marathons. When she washes my hair, I'm afraid I'll flash back to my hospitalization for blood clots. What if I slip up and call her "Nurse"? What if I flash *way* back and call her "Mommy"? What if she accidentally jabs me with the scissors like Andy did, and I start crying, and she mistakenly thinks she's hurt me, because why in the hell would anyone think that cutting hair is in any way related to cutting bodies? Why would anyone melt down in her chair unless something not dead has been damaged? What's an appropriate tip for someone I've enlisted as my unwitting trauma therapist? Two hundred percent?

It's weird to view a once-pleasurable and utterly ordinary activity as yet another shot at becoming the victim of human sacrifice.

The physical scar from my thyroid surgeries has faded, but clearly, my anxiety has not. I think I'd rather have it the other way around: a big, gnarly gash at my throat, still pink as the day it was made, and a barely perceptible fear response. Live big with my big gash, let people stare at it, let it represent the courage they hope they will have when they need it.

Even without chemo, I would be the cancer hero. Maybe then, I'd actually be brave enough to walk into Supercuts.

I don't push for marriage anymore. I figure if Andy changes his mind, if he wakes up and looks at me one morning and thinks, *Wife, yeah, that's the ticket,* he'll be sure to let me know.

Thankfully, people have stopped asking if we're tying the

knot or taking the plunge or what have you. Nineteen years together warrants a certain respect. Many marriages don't last that long.

But I know some people don't get it. I refer to Andy and he refers to me as "partner," and sometimes we get that telltale blink. Confusion: *What's with this "partner" crap?*

I'd like to tell them: We're not married. Not in the eyes of God or state or health coverage. But all of that seems beside the point. To me, marriage is no longer a way to define a relationship. It is no way to protect a relationship. No way to protect our lives.

Marriage won't magically preserve us both into our nineties. If it could, then maybe …

Now I want to be the one to tell the story of us. His body is not mine, but it is never without mine, not even when we're separated by miles, by days. We feel our mutual gravitation when Andy plays with his band in another city, or when I'm attending a writers' conference. We are not twins, but we travel through life much as twins do, our places in the cosmos defined by the position of the other. Our world is intensely private, understood only by us. It's not easy to explain all that we've been through together, or how it's strengthened the force of our bond.

I have pulled Andy too often into the path of illness. He has pulled me always into the path of health. *Our* health, his wonderfully stable well-being and my unpredictability that, after everything, has yielded many more good days than bad. When I get sick, chaos rocks our little universe. We are terrified when my light seems to dim.

He fears my next illness. I fear his first.

I am the light that answers his light, and he is the light that answers mine. Together we illuminate the way home.

I want to tell about this: When a man sits at your hospital bedside and weeps uncontrollably, clutching his face, gasping to get ahold of himself before the nurse comes back, when he says,

"You're my best friend, and I just can't imagine my life without you …"

… you're beyond married. "Husband" and "wife" cannot convey the reality of your existence. Only the story will do.

Acknowledgments

This book simply wouldn't exist without the support of the Postgraduate Writers' Conference at Vermont College of Fine Arts, which I attended annually for four years while I worked on *Mercy*. Gratitude to Sue William Silverman for turning to me at the end of a workshop and saying, "Marcia, you *must* write this book"; I can't imagine surviving this process without your continuing wisdom and love. Thank you to conference director Ellen Lesser for creating a true haven where writers can bring their doubts and struggles and come away exhilarated and renewed. Thanks to friends who cheered me on in the workshop and beyond: Elizabeth Kelsey, Judith Padow, Alice Bingham Gorman, Molly Barari, Shiv Dutta, Alison A. Ernst, Magin LaSov Gregg, and Margaret Whitford. I hope I've given you all as much as you've given me.

Much appreciation to Mike Ingram and Lilly Dancyger at Barrelhouse Books, for your amazing insights, expert judgment, and unwavering enthusiasm. Like all great editors, you saw things in my book that I didn't see, and you challenged me to work harder than I ever thought possible. I'm incredibly fortunate that you chose my manuscript. Working with you has been a true privilege.

Gratitude to my instructors at the Bennington Writing Seminars, for believing in me as a writer long before I believed in myself: Susan Cheever, George Packer, Sven Birkerts, and the late Lucy Grealy.

Thank you to my editing clients, for entrusting me with your stories, inspiring me with your talent and tenacity, and making me think about what it means to be a writer in chaotic times. I'm thrilled to share this book with you at long last.

And finally, endless thanks to my partner, Andy Greene, for reading draft after draft, taking over household chores so I could write, listening as I poured out my frustrations, and insisting that everything would work out just fine. I'm wildly grateful for your patience, devotion, and love.

Marcia Trahan is a native Vermonter, a freelance book editor, and a semiprofessional patient. She earned a bachelor of arts in psychology from the University of Vermont and a master of fine arts in writing and literature from Bennington College. Her essays and poetry have appeared in the *Brevity Blog*, *Fourth Genre*, *apt*, *Clare*, *Anderbo*, *Blood Orange Review*, *Connotation Press*, *Kansas City Voices*, and the LaChance Publishing anthology *Women Reinvented: True Stories of Empowerment and Change*. She lives in South Burlington, Vermont, with her partner, Andy, and their crazed feline companion, Bela.